Learn Hawaiian at Home

by Kahikāhealani Wight

3565 Harding Ave.
Honolulu, Hawaiʻi 96816
Phone: 1-800-910-2377
Fax: (808) 732-3627
www.besspress.com

Cover design: Carol Colbath
Illustrations: Wren
Design and production: Print Prep of Hawaii
CD Production coordinator: Caryl Nishioka

Library of Congress Cataloging-in-Publication Data

Wight, Kahikahealani.
Learn Hawaiian at home /
Kahikahealani Wight ; illustrated by
Wren.
p. cm.
Includes illustrations, glossaries.
ISBN 1-57306-245-6
1. Hawaiian language - Textbooks
for foreign speakers - English 2. Hawaiian
language - Spoken Hawaiian. I. Title.
PL6443.W54 2005   499.42-dc21

Printed by Sun Fung Offset Binding Company., Ltd., in China

Acknowledgments

The Hawaiian speakers on our *Learn Hawaiian at Home* CDs are Hauʻoli Akaka, Kalama Cabigon, Kaʻiulani Hoʻopai, Kaleo Kamai, "Tuti" Kanahele, Kuʻualohanui Kaulia, Mahina Kauakahi, Leinani Raffipiy, Melelani Nanihāʻupu Pang, Bill Panui, Larice Tam, and Kahikāhealani Wight.

Dunbar Wakayama and Kahikāhealani Wight are the English speakers.

Singing the songs is Kuʻuipo Kumukahi.

Mahalo nui to the Kanahele, Mitchell and Zuttermeister families and to Randie Fong and Puaʻala Nuʻuhiwa for allowing us to use their songs in this book.

Mahalo nui to Pierre Grill of Rendez-vous Recording Studio and to Dunbar Wakayama of Audio Media for their help in recording and editing the CDs.

Mahalo nui loa to Leinani Raffipiy for her attention to details, sound advice and support through many hours of shaping both text and CDs.

Table of Contents

Introduction to Learn Hawaiian at Home

Aloha nō kākou! E komo mai e 'ai! Aloha, everyone. Welcome to our home! Come in and eat with us! It is this traditional Hawaiian welcome that we would like to extend to our readers as we welcome you to our language, the heart and "home" of our culture. We wish to "feed" you with knowledge and aloha, so that your love for the Hawaiian culture may always grow. We hope that this book will stimulate you to seek more knowledge of our language and to play your part in the revival of our beloved **'ōlelo Hawai'i.**

The idea for this book arose from our awareness as Hawaiian language teachers of the many people who are interested in studying the language, but who must work full time and have difficulty in attending night classes. We then thought of visitors or people living outside of Hawai'i who might also be interested in a brief introduction to the language. Since it is not easy to find places to listen to Hawaiian, even in Hawai'i, we decided that recorded lessons would be a good way for students to gain feeling for Hawaiian intonation, pronunciation and phrasing.

This book is designed, then, as a brief introduction to the language with an emphasis on oral/aural learning. We feel that listening and speaking are of crucial importance to language learning. Thus, each chapter begins and ends with a variety of listening and speaking exercises.

THE ORAL WORK SECTION

The first section of each chapter has four parts: the **Hakalama** pronunciation chart, **Vocabulary** and **Useful Phrases,** then **Dialogs,** which give a preview of the grammar the chapter will deal with. All four parts are recorded so that you may listen to each part as often as you like. We also encourage you to practice saying each part of section one **out loud.**

Hawaiian pronunciation and spelling

Section one of each chapter begins with a variation of the **Hakalama** chart for pronunciation practice. The standard Hakalama chart, as presented in Chapter One, is a syllabic chart that originated in the early primers printed by the missionaries who taught Hawaiian adults to read and write in Hawaiian in the 1830s, '40s and '50s. If you read the chart from left to right, the first four syllables are **ha, ka, la** and **ma.**

Hence the name of the chart, which has been expanded in recent years to use in our Hawaiian language preschool and immersion programs to teach Hawaiian phonics. Rather than reading about how to pronounce Hawaiian, we prefer that you listen to and repeat the Hakalama.

When working on pronunciation it is important for you to remember a few basic rules of Hawaiian spelling. First of all, the Hawaiian alphabet has only thirteen letters: five vowels and eight consonants. Hawaiian consonants are H, K, L, M, N, P, W and the 'okina ('). The Hawaiian H is pronounced more strongly than in English; remember, there are no silent Hs in Hawaiian. W can be pronounced as a W or V or someplace in between, and will be pronounced differently by Hawaiians growing up in different parts of the islands. Listen to the last line of the Hakalama in Chapter 2 to hear different pronunciations of "w."

The 'okina is a glottal stop that occurs before vowels. Say "Oh Oh." Can you hear the break between the two "oh"s? That's an 'okina. When you see an 'okina, which looks like a backwards apostrophe, it's a signal to stop your voice and start again, to "cut off" or **'oki** the sound, so that the next vowel will be distinct.

In Hawaiian, as in other Polynesian languages, vowels are more important than consonants. This is one important difference between Hawaiian and English. In Hawaiian, vowels can stand alone and be words, but consonants can't. Each consonant must be followed by a vowel. Individual vowels must be pronounced **much more clearly** than in English. The duration of a vowel's sound can be lengthened by the addition of a mark, called a kahakō, over the vowel. The long mark over the **o** in **kahakō** lengthens the sound of the **o**, as if two **o**'s had been written. As a native speaker of English learning Hawaiian, you need to pay extra attention to all vowels! Listen carefully to the **Hakalama** and practice saying it out loud several times a day. There is an excellent pamphlet/cassette available for further study of Hawaiian pronunciation; it is listed in the **Conclusion.**

Next you will find a list of **vocabulary** words and **useful phrases** to be memorized. In choosing which words to include in our text, we have consulted the Department of Education's *Kupuna Program Teacher's Guide* and the *Hawaiian Word Book.* We have also used our own sense of what words are most culturally important and most practical. Where we had conflicts choosing between a culturally significant word or one of practical use, we chose the word that was of practical importance.

We have also listed more words in our **glossary** in the back of the book. We have deliberately limited the number of vocabulary words to be learned in this book to a few hundred. Obviously such a limited vocabulary will not make you fluent in Hawaiian. However, we believe that if you can learn sentence patterns and use the few words you know in full sentences, you will remember both the sentence patterns and the words themselves. Our goal is to have you speaking a simple, but correct Hawaiian when you have completed the book.

Next are two short **dialogs** that highlight the new sentence pattern to be learned in that chapter. The dialogs are examples of living language and demonstrate common, "everyday" greetings and questions. You can imitate them when you start your own Hawaiian conversations.

How to use flashcards

Buy colored index cards to use as flashcards to learn the new vocabulary. Use one color for nouns, another color for adjectives, yet another color for useful phrases, and so on. Carry each chapter's cards (with the Hawaiian on one side and the English on the other) with you throughout the day. Spend a few minutes at a time working with the cards as you stand in line at the bank, wait for the bus, and so forth. Say the Hawaiian word out loud, then say its English translation. Don't look at the English unless you're unsure of the meaning, Work as rapidly as you can, and repeat the process three or four times a day. Remember to say the words **out loud**; memorizing is easier if you use as many of your five senses as possible.

In addition to clearly distinguishing the parts of speech, color coding your flashcards will also prove helpful in learning the word order of Hawaiian sentences, which is different from that of English. English has a Subject Verb Object word order; that is, we usually hear the subject **first** in English. Hawaiian has a **Verb** Subject Object word order; in Hawaiian, we hear the subject **second.** When asked how you are, in English you respond: **I am well.** The Hawaiian translation literally says **good me:** maika'i au. Being able to construct sentences with the color-coded flashcards will make this key difference between the languages easier to grasp.

THE GRAMMAR SECTION

Section two of each chapter deals with grammar and constructing the five basic sentence patterns you will learn. Each chapter deals with one new sentence pattern, but several grammar points also need to be explained so that the new sentence pattern makes sense. For example, before learning how to ask and answer the question "What is your name?" you must learn the Hawaiian possessives **my, your, his/her.**

Since you have no teacher to ask questions of, we have attempted to explain the grammar as simply as possible. We have therefore chosen not to teach some of the more complicated points of Hawaiian grammar, such as the dual pronouns (as in the phrase **aloha kāua**, hello to you and me), for which there is no English equivalent. Also, we will not discuss "a-class" possessives (such as **ka'u, kāu, kāna**), although we will learn the singular "o-class" possessives (**ko'u, kou, kona**). The difference between the two kinds of possessives is confusing to beginning-level students even in a classroom setting. You will be understood if you use only "o-class" possessives, and learning the "a-class" possessives will be easier once you have the "o-class" forms down pat. In both the text and the answer key, words that are normally a-class possessives are marked with an asterisk (*).

Our goal in this book is to teach you enough to be able to carry on a simple conversation, because speaking makes Hawaiian a living language. We hope that those of you seeking a more in-depth syntactic explanation will be inspired to investigate other books (see our bibliography in the back) or to enroll in a class.

Each grammar section includes self-tests and homework, with answers in the answer section in the back of the book. Answer the questions of the self-test without looking up the answers, to see how much you remember. Then check the answers in the answer key. For the homework, refer to the text when necessary to complete the assignments. This middle section of each chapter is not on the CD.

THE ORAL REVIEW AND PRACTICE SECTION

The third section of each chapter is another series of oral exercises whose purpose is to reinforce the grammar you've just learned. This section has four parts: **Substitution Drills, Picture Practice, Listen and Learn**, and **Mele**. A few chapters also have English dialogs to translate.

This third section begins with oral **Substitution Drills.** You can listen and read along with the CD and later practice reading the drills out loud.

Next comes a picture for you to talk about, creating your own short dialog or story. We have also created a story about each picture, so that you can read and listen to more conversations about everyday activities. Throughout our book, we have chosen situations for our dialogs and stories that reflect Hawaiian culture as it is being lived today.

In the **Listen and Learn** section we learn about the different islands, beginning with Ni'ihau in the first chapter and progressing down the island chain to Hawai'i. The first story in this section is an exercise that will be repeated in each chapter with **only** the underlined words changed to tell about our new island. Because of the repetition and simplicity of the story, it will be easy to memorize. Next we give you a listening challenge with a more complex story about our subject island.

Finally, each chapter ends with a **mele,** or song, for the island featured in the **Listen and Learn** section. You can read the words and sing along with the CD. Hawaiian songs are our poetry, and singing songs is a fun and exciting way to learn the language.

How to Use This Book

Every language learner has different degrees of skill in reading, writing, comprehension and speaking, and each learns these separate language skills in ways that are different from other learners'. We have tried to accommodate different modes of learning as well as different degrees of interest by building some flexibility into our book. Although we believe that the best way to learn is to go through each chapter from start to finish, there are many different ways to learn from each chapter.

If you would like to have a brief "taste" of what Hawaiian sounds like, you may listen to the CD without looking at the book. Another way to "taste" Hawaiian is to work only on the **Listen and Learn** section at the end of each chapter. This section will teach you how to correctly pronounce the name of each island and its main town as well as provide you with other cultural information. Also, you can easily memorize the "individual island" exercise. This will help train your ear to Hawaiian intonation and help you learn Hawaiian phrasing, that is, which groups of words belong together in a sentence. For ,a musical "taste" of

Hawaiian, learn and sing along with the songs in praise of the individual islands. Songs display the strong urge Hawaiian speakers have for subtle and poetic expressions of feeling; it is the combination of their love for poetry and music that makes songs so meaningful to many Hawaiians. Learning to chant, dance or sing at least a few songs is an integral part of learning the language.

If you would like a slightly bigger "bite" and want to concentrate on Hawaiian pronunciation, you may listen to the **Hakalama** exercise in each chapter. After listening to the Hakalama on CD, read it out loud a few times daily for practice. Work on one variation of the Hakalama until you are very comfortable saying it out loud before moving on to the next chapter. Because the exercises become progressively more difficult in each chapter, it is important to work with them in sequence.

In order to make our text easier to use, we have substituted symbols for some instructions that are frequently repeated. If you are to listen to the recording of a section, you will see a CD symbol on the page. If you are to use flashcards for an exercise, we have included a flashcard symbol on the page.

If you are to check your own homework in the answer key, a key symbol is included after the homework instructions. Refer to the answer key for that chapter to find the answers to Homework and Self-Test exercises.

How to Study

The serious student who wants to really "digest" the language needs a few directions on how to study **Learn Hawaiian at Home**. You will need daily practice on all four language skills discussed above. Repeat the Hakalama out loud several times a day for pronunciation practice. Learn vocabulary and useful phrases with color-coded flashcards. Listen to the CD if you need to hear the vocabulary or useful phrases again. Saying the words **out loud** is good ear training as well as a great help for memorization.

Spend 10 to 15 minutes daily on both pronunciation and vocabulary practice. Spend another concentrated 15 minutes daily on grammar. Always wait until you have read the grammar explanation before doing the Self-Test exercises or Homework. Answers to Self-Test and Homework exercises are in the Answer section at the back of the book.

The **ORAL REVIEW AND PRACTICE** (the last) section of each chapter is the most complex because we are using full sentences and a more advanced level of language than in the **ORAL WORK** section. Spend 10 minutes a day on the substitution drills; after repeated practice using the CDs, make up your own words to substitute in each phrase. Spend five minutes a day going over one other part of this last chapter section: work on singing one day, on the **Listen and Learn** story the next, and so on. Remember to focus your practice on listening and speaking **out loud.**

Be creative with your approach to our book and CDs. Mix and match written work, reading, listening. Choose the part of each chapter that appeals to you the most. If you like, concentrate just on the songs. Use **Learn Hawaiian at Home** to learn a lot or a little, to have a small "taste" of our language or to "eat" a full meal. We hope that you will learn to love our beautiful language and be inspired to speak it, so that it remains a living language.

E ola ka ʻōlelo Hawaiʻi! May the Hawaiian language live!

Chapter One

GREETINGS, OR WHAT TO SAY AFTER YOU SAY ALOHA

I. ORAL WORK SECTION

a. Hakalama

Here is the standard Hakalama pronunciation chart. Read it out loud going across the line. Recite the Hakalama several times a day for practice. (Remember that the long mark over the vowel, the kahakō, lengthens the sound, as if the vowel were doubled.)

Ha Ka La Ma Na Pa Wa ʻĀ
He Ke Le Me Ne Pe We ʻĒ
Hi Ki Li Mi Ni Pi Wi ʻĪ
Ho Ko Lo Mo No Po Wo ʻŌ
Hu Ku Lu Mu Nu Pu Wu ʻŪ

Hā Kā Lā Mā Nā Pā Wā ʻĀ
Hē Kē Lē Mē Nē Pē Wē ʻĒ
Hī Kī Lī Mī Nī Pī Wī ʻĪ
Hō Kō Lō Mō Nō Pō Wō ʻŌ
Hū Kū Lū Mū Nū Pū Wū ʻŪ

b. Vocabulary

Listen to the CD and repeat these words aloud. Make flashcards to help yourself learn the words. Use colored index cards. **Nouns** are orange, **adjectives** green. Be sure to use one color for nouns and a different color for adjectives. Do <u>not</u> write **ke** or **ka** on the flashcard for nouns; instead, guess which is correct with each noun.

Nouns		Adjectives	
ke **akua**	god	**maikaʻi**	good, well, fine
ke **kanaka**	human	**ʻoluʻolu**	kind, comfortable
ka **lani**	heaven, chief	**māluhiluhi**	tired
ka **honua**	earth	**maʻi**	sick, ill
ka **wahine**	woman, wife	**hohono**	bad-smelling
ke **kāne**	man, husband	**ʻaʻala**	fragrant, sweet-smelling
ka **inoa**	name	**nui**	big
ka **ʻohana**	family	**liʻiliʻi**	little
ke **kupuna**	grandparent	**kahiko**	old
ka **moʻopuna**	grandchild	**hou**	new
ka **makua**	parent	**kaumaha**	heavy, sad
ke **keiki**	child	**hauʻoli**	happy
ke **aloha**	love	**nani**	pretty
ka **hoaaloha**	friend	**pupuka**	ugly
ke **kula**	school	**momona**	sweet-tasting, fat

ka **haumāna**	student	**wīwī**	thin
ke **kumu**	teacher	**lōʻihi**	tall
ka **ʻōlelo**	language, speech	**pōkole**	short

Note: **Ka** <u>wahine</u> means "**the** woman." <u>Ke</u> <u>kāne</u> means "**the** man." The rules for choosing either **ke** or **ka** to translate "the" are explained in this chapter. Remember that <u>wahine</u> means "woman," <u>kāne</u> means "man," and that other words can replace "the" before a noun; for example, **<u>kēia</u>** <u>kāne</u> means "**this** man."

c. Useful Phrases

Read these phrases as you listen to them on the CD; then say them out loud several times by yourself. Make flashcards to help memorize these phrases as well. Make them blue or some other color to distinguish them from nouns or adjectives.

Aloha kākou	Greetings to all of us (3 or more).
Aloha kāua	Greetings to both of us (you and me).
Aloha kakahiaka	Good morning (6 a.m. to 10 a.m.).
Aloha awakea	Good noontime (10 a.m. to 2 p.m.).
Aloha ʻauinalā	Good afternoon (2 p.m. to 6 p.m.).
Aloha ahiahi	Good evening (6 p.m. to 10 p.m.).**
Aloha kakahiaka kākou	Good morning to us all.
Aloha ahiahi kāua	Good evening to both of us.
ʻAe	Yes.
ʻAʻole	No.
Pehea ʻoe?	How are you?
Maikaʻi nō au, mahalo.	I'm very well, thanks.
Māluhiluhi au.	I'm tired.
Maʻi ʻo ia.	Sheʻis sick.
Aloha kāua, e ke kumu.	Hello to you and me, teacher.
Aloha ahiahi, e Momi.	Good evening, Momi.
Aloha kakahiaka kākou, e ka papa	Good morning to us all, class.

Note that in Hawaiian thinking, "morning" covers the hours up to 10 a.m.; then "noontime" lasts from 10 a.m. to 2 p.m. During those noon hours we say "good noontime," **aloha awakea, rather than **aloha kakahiaka.** After 2 p.m. we switch to "good afternoon," **aloha ʻauinalā,** until 6 p.m.

Note also that these time periods are generally followed, but they are not always strictly adhered to, especially among native speakers.

Self-Test 1-1

Which greeting is correct at each of the times listed below? Choose from **aloha kakahiaka, aloha awakea, aloha 'auinalā, aloha ahiahi.** Check your answers in the answer key section.

1. 8:10 a.m.	5. 7:13 p.m.	9. 5:30 p.m.
2. 11:25 a.m.	6. 10:50 a.m.	10. 9:34 a.m.
3. 1:45 p.m.	7. 6:05 p.m.	11. 12:04 p.m.
4. 3 p.m.	8. 2:20 p.m.	12. 9 p.m.

In Hawaiian thinking, politeness means extending greetings to all those present, including the person speaking. We do this by adding the pronoun **kākou** (us all) or **kāua** (you and me) to the end of our "**aloha,**" whether we are saying "hello" or referring to a specific time of day. **Kākou** is used when three or more people are present, including the speaker. **Kāua** includes only two people, the person speaking and the person spoken to. For example, **Aloha kāua** is used to say "Hello" in answering the telephone. Remember that when we add these pronouns to our "good morning," "good noontime," "good afternoon" or "good evening," **kāua** or **kākou** must be added to the end of the greeting, as in "**aloha awakea kākou.**"

Self-Test 1-2

Matching. Write the number of the Hawaiian greeting next to the correct translation.

1. Aloha ahiahi, e Momi.	__ Good noontime everyone.
2. Aloha 'auinalā.	__ Hello to all of us.
3. Aloha kāua, e ko'u hoaaloha.	__ Good evening, Momi.
4. Aloha kakahiaka kākou.	__ Hello, teacher.
5. Aloha awakea kāua.	__ Good morning, Kainalu.
6. Aloha, e ke kumu.	__ Good afternoon.
7. Aloha kākou.	__ Hello to both of us, my friend.
8. Aloha kakahiaka, e Kainalu.	__ Good morning to all of us.
9. Aloha ahiahi kāua.	__ Good noontime to you and me.
10. Aloha awakea kākou.	__ Good evening to you and me.

Homework 1-1

 Translate the following greetings.

1. Good noontime.
2. Good morning.
3. Hello to you and me.
4. Good evening to us all.
5. Good afternoon to you and me.
6. Good morning everyone.
7. Good evening to you and me.
8. Hello everyone.
9. Good noontime to us all.
10. Good evening.

d. Dialogs

 Listen to the CD recording of these conversations and read along as you listen. After listening a few times, read them out loud. If you have a partner, you can each read a different part.

1. <u>Kamaʻilio ke kumu me ka haumāna.</u>
Ke kumu: Aloha kakahiaka, e ka haumāna.
Ka haumāna: ʻAe, aloha kakahiaka, e ke kumu.
Ke kumu: E ka haumāna, pehea ʻoe?
Ka haumāna: Maikaʻi nō au, mahalo. A ʻo ʻoe, pehea ʻoe?
Ke kumu: Māluhiluhi au.

The teacher talks with the student.
Teacher: Good morning, student.
Student: Yes, good morning, teacher.
Teacher: Student, how are you?
Student: I'm very well, thanks. And you, how are you?
Teacher: I'm tired.

2. Kama'ilio 'o Kaipo me Kanani.
Kaipo: E Kanani, aloha 'auinalā kāua!
Kanani: Aloha 'auinalā, e Kaipo! Pehea kou 'ohana?
Kaipo: Maika'i ko'u 'ohana. Hau'oli lākou.
Kanani: Pehea kou kupuna? Ma'i 'o ia?
Kaipo: 'A'ole. Maika'i ko'u kupuna.

Kaipo talks to Kanani.
Kaipo: Kanani, good afternoon to you and me.
Kanani: Good afternoon, Kaipo. How's your family?
Kaipo: My family is well. They are happy.
Kanani: How is your grandparent? Is he sick?
Kaipo: No. My grandparent is fine.

II. GRAMMAR SECTION

a. Pronouns

These are the Hawaiian **singular** pronouns:

1. **wau, au**   I

> **Wau** and **au** are interchangeable; some Hawaiian speakers choose whichever sounds nicest in a particular sentence.

2. **'oe**   **you**

> **'Oe** refers to one person only.

3. **'o ia**   **he, she**

> **'O ia** does not indicate whether the person being spoken about is male or female, although we can usually tell from context.

These are the Hawaiian **plural** pronouns:

kākou	**we, all of us**
'oukou	**you all**
lākou	**they, them**

Note that the plural pronouns refer to at least three people. Hawaiian has a separate set of pronouns to refer to two people, such as the greeting "**Aloha kāua,**" "Hello to you and me." The pronoun system in Hawaiian, as in other Polynesian languages, is more precise and more complicated than in English. In this book we will limit ourselves to the pronouns listed above, since they are similar to those used in English.

Pronouns Self-Test 1-3

 Draw a line from the English pronoun to the Hawaiian translation.

she	**lākou**
I	**'oe**
we all	**'o ia**
he	**'oukou**
you all	**'o ia**
they all	**wau, au**
you (singular)	**kākou**

Homework 1-2

Read the English sentence; then fill in the blank in the Hawaiian translation with the correct singular or plural pronoun.

1. She is sick.	Maʻi_____.
2. I am nice.	ʻOluʻolu_____.
3. They are fine.	Maikaʻi_____.
4. Mehana, are you happy?	E Mehana, hauʻoli_____?
5. He is tired.	Māluhiluhi_____.
6. We all are well.	Maikaʻi_____.
7. Yes, I am happy.	ʻAe, hauʻoli_____.
8. You all are kind.	ʻOluʻolu_____.
9. Are they tired?	Māluhiluhi_____?
10. Is she sick?	Maʻi_____?

Did you notice that asking a question **(Is she sick?)** and making a statement **(She is sick.)** have the **same** translation? The only difference is in intonation.

b. Noun Announcers

In Hawaiian, every **noun** must be preceded by a **noun announcer.** The **noun announcer** does precisely what its name says; it tells us "here comes a noun." In English, we can leave out the noun announcer at times, such as when we address someone by his or her title: **"Teacher, how are you?"** or when we talk about an institution: "I go to **church** on Tuesday." In Hawaiian, we translate these sentences by literally saying "Hey **the** teacher, how are you?" and "I go to **the** church on **the** Tuesday."

Teacher, how are you?	E **ke** kumu, pehea ʻoe?
I go to church on Tuesday.	Hele au i **ka** halepule ma **ka** pōʻalua.

Noun announcers are called demonstratives and possessives in English, words like **the, this, that, my, your, their.** In Hawaiian, noun announcers are numerous and so frequently used that you will soon memorize them.

1. **ke** or **ka:** which word for **the**?

Go back over the nouns in your vocabulary list. You will notice that both **ke** and **ka** are used to translate **the. Ka** is the most commonly used, for about 80 percent of Hawaiian words. If you have to guess whether to use **ke** or **ka** to translate "the," guess **ka**. **Ke** is the noun announcer used before words that begin with the letters **k, a, e, o,** such as **ke k**ula, **ke a**lanui, **ke e**a or **ke o**la. All other words take **ka** (with a few exceptions like **ke** po'o). The only tricky situation is a word that begins with an 'okina: these words take **ka,** such as **ka** 'ehukai, **ka** 'a'ama and **ka** 'olelo.

Self-Test 1-4 for **ke** or **ka**

Write **ke** or **ka** in the blank in front of each word. How did you know which one to choose?

1. _____kāne	6. _____kaikamahine
2. _____wahine.	7. _____ala
3. _____aloha	8. _____makua
4. _____kupuna	9. _____imu
5. _____hale	10. _____'opihi

2. kēia and kēlā: this and that

Maika'i **kēia** kula.   **This** school is good.
'Olu'olu **kēlā** hale?   Is **that** building comfortable?

Kēia is the noun announcer that translates **this**. **Kēlā** translates **that**. Since all noun announcers can substitute for each other, you can practice them by using your noun flashcards.

Self-Test 1-5

Hold up a noun card and say it out loud with the appropriate word for *the* (**ke** or **ka**). Then substitute **kēia** or **kēlā**.

Translate into English. For example, take the word **makuakāne,** father. Say **ka** makuakāne, **kēia** makuakāne, **kēlā** makuakāne; **the** father, **this** father, **that** father.

3. ko'u, kou, kona: my, your, his/her

Nani **kou** hale!   **Your** house is pretty!
Ma'i **kona** makuakāne?   Is **her** father ill?
Maika'i **ko'u** kula.   **My** school is good.

These noun announcers are the possessive forms for the singular pronouns. Only the 'okina separates **ko'u** from **kou;** the difference

between **my** and **your** is that because **I'm** special, things that are mine
are indicated with an extra syllable. Practice saying **ko'u** makuahine,
then **kou** makuahine several times. Another way in which Hawaiian dif-
fers from English is that **kou** refers only to a single person's things,
while the English word **your** can refer to something belonging to one,
several or many persons. Be aware, then, that the noun announcer **kou**
will not translate all the meanings of **your**. Remember that **kona** refers
to either a male or female possessor and can be translated as **his** or
her. Again, context will usually help you decide which sex owns the
noun.

Self-Test 1-6

Matching. Write the number of the English phrase next to
its Hawaiian translation.

1. her school	__ kona hale
2. his house	__ ko'u halepule
3. your friend	__ kona* kumu
4. my grandparent	__ kou makuahine
5. her father	__ kona ali'i
6. your mother	__ ko'u kupuna
7. my church	__ kona makuakāne
8. his teacher	__ kou aloha
9. your love	__ kou hoaaloha
10. her chief	__ kona kula

Read the Hawaiian phrases in the above Self-Test out loud. Then take
each noun and substitute all the noun announcers you know for the
possessive noun announcer. This can be a written as well as an oral
practice.

Homework 1-3

Fill in the blanks with the correct noun announcer.

1. his student	____ haumāna
2. your friend	____ hoaaloha
3. that mother	____ makuahine
4. this store	____ halekū'ai
5. my love	____ aloha
6. this woman	____ wahine

7. her building	___ hale
8. that 'opihi	___ 'opihi
9. his father	___ makuakāne
10. your grandparent	___ kupuna

Homework 1-4

 Translate the following phrases into Hawaiian.

1. that school_____
2. my church _____
3. this store _____
4. her love _____
5. your husband _____
6. the imu _____
7. your teacher _____
8. that student _____
9. his hat _____
10. the house _____

Homework 1-5

Translate the following dialogs from English into Hawaiian.

1.   Good evening. _____
     Hello to both of us. _____
     How are you? _____
     I'm tired! How are you? _____
     I'm fine. _____

2.   Good afternoon to all of us! _____
     Yes, good afternoon. _____
     How's school? _____
     School is fine. We're all happy. _____
     Good! See you later. _____
     Yes. Goodbye 'til we meet again. _____

III. ORAL REVIEW AND PRACTICE - DRILLS, DIALOGS, STORIES

a. Substitution Drills

In each of the following phrases, substitute the words listed for the underlined words. Listen to the CD for an example; then practice out loud on your own.

Aloha kāua, e **ka haumāna**.
    ke kāne.
    Kuʻulei.
    koʻu hoaaloha.
    ke kumu.
    Nālani.

Aloha kakahiaka, e ka wahine.
Aloha ʻauinalā
Aloha awakea
Aloha kāua
Aloha ahiahi
Aloha nō

Pehea **ʻoe**, e Kaleilani?
    ke kula
    kēlā hoaaloha
    kou* keiki
    kēia hale
    kona* haumāna

Maikaʻi nō au, mahalo.
Māluhiluhi
Hauʻoli nō
Maʻi
Kaumaha
ʻOluʻolu

Pehea **kākou**?
    ʻo ia?
    kāua?
    lākou?
    ʻoukou?
    ʻoe?
    wau?

ʻOluʻolu **kāua**.
 koʻu kupuna.
ʻo ia.
kona* kumu.
lākou.
ke kanaka.
ʻoukou.

For an extra challenge, listen to the CD without looking at the book. Do you understand everything? Can you transcribe (write down) what you hear?

b. Picture Practice

1. Look at the picture below. Make up a story to go along with the picture. What are the names of the people? How are they related? What do they say to each other?

2. We have made up a story about Kaipo Kealoha and his mother greeting Kaipo's teacher on the first day of school. Cover up the English translation and read the Hawaiian while you listen to the CD. Next, listen to the CD alone. Do you understand? If not, refer to the translation.

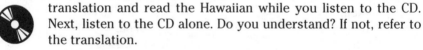

'O kēia ka lā mua i ke kula. Aia 'o Kaipo Kealoha me kona makuahine i ke kula. Ke kama'ilio nei lāua me ke kumu.

Ka makuahine: Aloha kakahiaka, e ke kumu. 'O Kaipo kēia.
Ke kumu: 'Ae, aloha kakahiaka kākou. E Kaipo, pehea kou
    makuahine?
Kaipo: Maika'i ko'u makuahine, e ke kumu.
Ke kumu: A 'o 'oe, pehea 'oe, e ke keiki?
Kaipo: Hau'oli nō au, e ke kumu.
Ke kumu: Maika'i.
Kaipo: Aloha a hui hou, e Māmā.
Ka makuahine: 'Ae, a hui hou, e Kaipo.

This is the first day at school. Kaipo Kealoha and his mother are at school. They are talking with the teacher.

Mother: Good morning, teacher. This is Kaipo.
Teacher: Yes, good morning to us all. Kaipo, how's your mother?
Kaipo: My mother is fine, teacher.
Teacher: And you, how are you, child?
Kaipo: I'm really happy, teacher.
Teacher: That's good.
Kaipo: See you later, Mom.
Mother: Yes, see you later, Kaipo.

c. **Listen and Learn**
Listen to the CD and read along to learn about our 'āina. This story
will be repeated in each chapter with only the underlined words
changed as we talk about the different islands. This gives you a
chance to memorize a simple story about each island and to learn
that island's color, lei, mountain and famous chief. Let's start with
Ni'ihau.

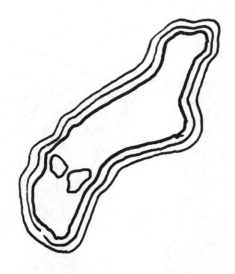

'O Ni'ihau kēia mokupuni 'O Pu'uwai ke kūlanakauhale. He ke'oke'o ka
waiho'olu'u no Ni'ihau, He lei pūpū kona lei. 'O Kahelelani ke ali'i
kaulana no Ni'ihau. 'O Pānī'au ke kuahiwi nani.

This island is Ni'ihau. Pu'uwai is the town. The color of Ni'ihau is
white. Its lei is the shell lei. The famous chief of Ni'ihau is Kahelelani.
The beautiful mountain is Pānī'au.

As a further listening challenge, we offer a more difficult story about each island. Listen along with the CD.

Ua kaulana nā lei pūpū o Niʻihau. No Niʻihau wale nō kēia ʻano lei. Nui nā waihoʻoluʻu o nā pūpū liʻiliʻi a nui nō hoʻi nā inoa o nā pūpū. ʻO Kahelelani ka inoa o kekahi ʻano pūpū. ʻO Kahelelani ke aliʻi kaulana o Niʻihau i ka wā kahiko. ʻŌlelo Hawaiʻi ka poʻe o Niʻihau a hīmeni lākou no nā pūpū nani o ko lākou ʻāina.

The shell leis of Niʻihau are famous. This kind of lei is only from Niʻihau. There are many colors of the small shells and also many names for the shells. Kahelelani is the name of one kind of shell. Kahelelani was the famous chief of Niʻihau in the ancient times. The people of Niʻihau speak Hawaiian and they sing about the beautiful shells of their land.

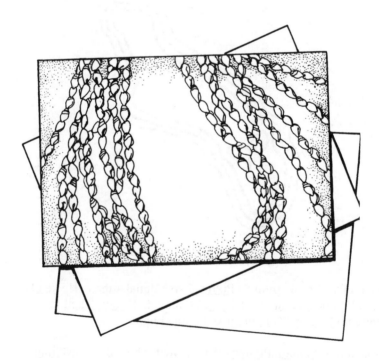

d. Mele

Here is a well-known song for Niʻihau. Learn the words and sing along with the CD.

This song speaks to the shells of Niʻihau and asks them to show their beauty. It also tells of someoneʻs fond memories of his or her sweetheart.

Pūpū O Niʻihau,
composed by the Kanahele family of Niʻihau

Pūpū o Niʻihau,
ʻAuhea ʻoe?
Hōʻike aʻe ʻoe
a i kou nani

He nani hiehie
ʻoi kelakela
Ka ʻiʻini nui ia
o kuʻu puʻuwai

Hō mai kou aloha
a pili me aʻu
i koʻolua noho
kahi mehameha

I luna māua
aʻo Hāʻupu
Upu aʻe ke aloha
nou e ka ipo

Haʻina ʻia mai
ana ka puana
Pūpū o Niʻihau
ʻAuhea ʻoe?

Chapter Two

DESCRIPTIVE SENTENCE PATTERN

I. ORAL WORK SECTION

a. Hakalama

Here is the first variation on the Hakalama pronunciation chart. Notice that we are now reading vertically down the columns. Listen to the CD and practice saying the syllables out loud.

Ha He Hi Ho Hu	Hā Hē Hī Hō Hū
Ka Ke Ki Ko Ku	Kā Kē Kī Kō Kū
La Le Li Lo Lu	Lā Lē Lī Lō Lū
Ma Me Mi Mo Mu	Mā Mē Mī Mō Mū
Na Ne Ni No Nu	Nā Nē Nī Nō Nū
Pa Pe Pi Po Pu	Pā Pē Pī Pō Pū
Wa We Wi Wo Wu	Wā Wē Wī Wō Wū

Try doubling the syllables for a practice variation. Say **Haha, Hehe, Hihi, Hoho, Huhu** and so on. Another variation: what happens when you mix the syllables? Say **Hahe, Hahi, Haho, Hahu, Heha, Hehi** and so on. What other variations can you come up with? Saying them out loud gives good training to mouth muscles that must move in new ways now. At the same time, you are helping to train your ears to tune in to Hawaiian sounds.

b. Vocabulary

Make flashcards as discussed in the introductory chapter. **Nouns** are orange, **adjectives** green. Do not include the **ka/ke** noun announcer on your noun flashcards; practice using all **noun announcers** with each noun.

Nouns		Adjectives	
ke **aliʻi**	chief, royalty	**anuanu**	cold
ka **makaʻāinana**	commoner	**wela**	hot
ke **kai**	sea	**ikaika**	strong
ka **ʻāina**	land	**nāwaliwali**	weak
ke **kupunakāne**	grandfather	**akamai**	smart
ke **kupunawahine**	grandmother	**naʻaupō**	ignorant
ka **pēpē**	baby	**ʻāwīwī**	quick
ka **mokupuni**	island	**lohi**	slow
ke **kuahiwi**	mountain	**kokoke**	near (distance)

→

ka **lā**	sun, day	**mamao**	far (distance)
ka **māka'i**	policeman	**mālie**	calm
ka **hale**	house, building	**'ino**	stormy, bad
ka **halemāka'i**	police station	**ola**	healthy
ka **ha'awina**	lesson, homework	**pau**	finished, destroyed
ka **puke**	book	**hala**	passed by, dead
ke **ki'i**	picture, image	**maka'u**	afraid
ka **lolouila**	computer	**koa**	courageous
ka **pepa**	paper	**kaulana**	famous
ka **papa**	class	**hanohano**	distinguished

c. Useful Phrases

Wela **ka** lā.	The sun is hot.
Wela **kēia** lā.	Today is hot./It's hot today.
Wela **'o** Kalā.	Kalā is hot.
Wela **ke** kālā.	The money is hot.
ka lā wela	the hot sun, the hot day
Akamai **ke** kauka.	The doctor is smart.
Akamai **'o** Kauka.	Kauka is smart.
Akamai **'o ia**.	She is smart.
kēlā kauka akamai	that smart doctor
ko'u hale 'olu'olu	my comfortable house
Aloha nō!	Too bad! How sad!
A hui hou!	See you later!
Aloha a hui hou!	Goodbye 'til we meet again!
E mālama pono!	Take care!

d. Dialogs

1. <u>Kama'ilio 'o Kau'i me kona hoaaloha hou, 'o Kealoha.</u>
Kau'i: Aloha awakea, e Kealoha.
Kealoha: 'Ae, aloha nō. Pehea ke kula, e Kau'i?
Kau'i: Maika'i ke kula. 'Olu'olu nō ke kumu.
Kealoha: Auē! Hau'oli ka papa, 'eā?

Kau'i talks with her new friend, Kealoha.
Kau'i: Good noontime, Kealoha.
Kealoha: Yes, hello indeed. How's school, Kau'i?
Kau'i: School's good. The teacher is very nice.
Kealoha: Wow! The class is happy, huh?

2. Kama'ilio ka wahine me kona kupunakāne.
Ka wahine: Wela kēia lā, e Tūtū.
Ke Kupunakāne: 'Ae, wela no. Nāwaliwali kou kupunawahine.
Ka wahine: Auē! Aloha nō. Kaumaha 'o ia?
Ke Kupunakāne: 'A'ole. Wela nō 'o ia!
Ka wahine: 'A'ole maika'i kēia wela. E mālama pono!

<u>The woman talks with her grandfather.</u>
The woman: It's hot today, Grampa.
The grandfather: Yes, it's really hot. Your grandmother is weak.
The woman: Gosh! Too bad! Is she sad?
The grandfather: No. She's very hot!
The woman: This heat isn't good. Take care!

II. GRAMMAR SECTION

a. Parts of the Hawaiian Sentence: Head and Center

The simple Hawaiian sentence has two main parts: the **Head** and the **Center**.

HEAD	CENTER
Nani	**'o ia.**
Nani	kēia lā.
Nani	'o Kalā.
Nani	kona makuahine.

Note that each part can contain one or more words. Let's focus first on the center section. The **Center** section tells who or what the sentence is about. There are three different kinds of subjects found in the center of Hawaiian sentences.

b. Three Kinds of Center Subjects

Pronouns are the simplest type of subject, because they have just one word in the center. Review the pronouns you learned in the last chapter. How many singular pronouns do you know? How many plural? Say all of them with the same descriptive word in the **Head** position.

HEAD	CENTER	
Hau'oli	**wau.**	I am happy.
Hau'oli	**kāua?**	Are we (**you and I**) happy?
Hau'oli	**kākou.**	We (**all**) are happy.

Self-Test 2-1

Which pronouns did we leave out? Make them happy, too.

Homework 2-1

Pick just one green **adjective** flashcard, for example **mālie.**
Say the **adjective** out loud; then add a **pronoun** as the Center
subject. What do the sentences you've made say? Who's **mālie?** Make
all the pronouns **mālie.** (Remember that you have to memorize the
pronouns: repeat them from memory as you create your sentences.)

The second kind of subject is the **name of a place or a person.** In the
Center position, all names must be preceded by **ʻo.** This word is not
translated into English, but must be present in Hawaiian. Remember
our discussion of **noun** announcer words? You can think of **ʻo** as the
<u>name</u> announcer, if you like. No **name** can appear in the **Center** with-
out its **name announcer!**

HEAD	CENTER	
Kaulana	**ʻo** Kaipo.	Kaipo is famous.
Kaulana	**ʻo** Waiʻanae.	Waiʻanae is famous.
Kaulana	**ʻo** ʻAnakē Lehua.	Aunty Lehua is famous.
Kaulana	**ʻo** Kaʻū.	Kaʻū is famous.

Notice that Waiʻanae and Kaʻū are place names and they also require
a **name announcer,** just as people's names do.

Self-Test 2-2

Compare and contrast the following pair of sentences. How are they
alike? Explain the difference in meaning.

Nani ka pua.	The flower is pretty.
Nani **ʻo** Kapua.	Kapua is pretty.

The distinction between the two sentences above is the **name
announcer.** Without the **name** announcer, the **Center** in the second
sentence is not complete. Remember that **all** names (names of streets,
mountains, buildings, songs, and so forth) <u>must</u> have a **name
announcer** in front of them.

Homework 2-2

Think of five place names in Hawai'i. Pick out one green **adjective** flashcard, such as **hanohano,** to start a sentence about the first place. Continue making sentences until you've made each place "**hanohano.**" Repeat with five names of people you know. Write these ten sentences down. Circle the **Center** and underline the **Head** in each sentence.

The third type of subject is the **noun announcer plus noun** combination. How many **noun announcers** do you know from the greetings chapter? Say aloud five that you can recall from memory.** Choose one new noun from this chapter and recite all the possible noun announcer words that can go in front of it. What word will you use for "the"? Review the rules for choosing **ke** or **ka.** Why is it **ke** <u>kauka</u>, but not **ke** <u>lawai'a?</u> What do **kēia** kauka and **kēlā** lawai'a mean? What do **kona** hale and **kou** ka'a mean?

HEAD	CENTER	
Ikaika	**kēlā** wahine.	That woman is strong.
Ikaika	**kou** makuakāne?	Is your father strong?
Ikaika	**ke** kula.	School is strong.
Ikaika	**kona** ka'a.	Her (his) car is strong.

Remember that without a **noun announcer** your **noun** is "naked" and the **Center** is not complete. Without a **noun announcer,** the meaning of your sentence is lost. Just as each **place name** or **personal name** must be preceded by a **name announcer,** so also each **noun** must be preceded by a **noun announcer.**

These should include **kēia, kēlā, ke or **ka, ko'u, kou** and **kona.**

Homework 2-3

Here are words that would like to become **Center** subjects. However, each is incomplete and can't be used as a Center. Complete them so that they can be used. What did you add?

1. Moloka'i	4. Nāihe	7. Lā'ie	10. Wailau
2. kaikamahine	5. halekula	8. kumu	11. aloha
3. kāne	6. hoaaloha	9. imu	12. kupunawahine

Homework 2-4

Below are some possible **Center** subjects. Circle the ones that are not complete and explain why they can't be used.

1. Lānaʻi	5. Keola	9. ʻo Mehana
2. lākou	6. ke wahine	10. lawaiʻa
3. hale	7. ʻo ia	11. ka pāpale
4. kou hoaaloha	8. kēia kumu	12. Waiʻaleʻale

c. Descriptive Sentence Pattern

Our first sentence pattern is based on the **Pehea ʻoe? Maikaʻi nō au** question and answer learned in our first chapter on greetings. The response "I'm fine" describes how you feel. Review other responses you have learned. What if you were sad, tall or purple? You tell us about yourself with this same kind of sentence. Is your house big, old and comfortable? Use a **descriptive** sentence to tell us a **trait, quality, or characteristic** of any person, place or thing.

Nani nō ʻo Hāna.	Hāna is <u>really beautiful</u>.
Liʻiliʻi kēia halekūʻai.	This store is <u>small</u>.
ʻOluʻolu ʻo ia.	She is <u>kind</u>. (or) He is <u>kind</u>.
ʻOluʻolu kou halekula?	Is your school building <u>comfortable</u>?
Wela nō kēia lā!	Today is <u>very hot</u>!

Self-Test 2-3

Look at the Hawaiian sentences above. What is each sentence talking about? Circle the Center in each sentence. What is said about the Center? Underline the descriptive word in each sentence.

Self-Test 2-4

Look at the following English sentences. What is each sentence talking about? Circle the subject in these sentences. What is said about that subject? Underline the descriptive word in each sentence.

1. Kīlauea (a place name) is cold.
2. Your grandmother is tall.
3. This island is pretty.
4. Mēlia is slow.
5. The chief is smart.

How do you make a **descriptive** sentence? Begin with an **adjective** in the **Head** or first part of the sentence. How do you say Puanani is small? **Li'ili'i 'o Puanani.** Sometimes you will add **nō** after the descriptive word for emphasis. **Nō** can be translated "very, indeed, really." You already know what can go in the **Center.** How do you say Puanani is very happy? **Hau'oli nō 'o Puanani.**

HEAD: adjective	**CENTER**
Nani nō	'o Puanani.
Māluhiluhi	ka haumāna
Anuanu	kākou

How do you say Puanani is healthy? quick? courageous? You are telling us a characteristic, quality, or trait about who or what is in the **Center.**

Homework 2-5

Start with a green flashcard; then pick any orange noun flashcard to complete your sentence. What **noun announcer** did you use? Practice changing your **noun announcer** word in each sentence you create. Don't make flashcards for the noun announcer words: you must memorize them! Write down ten sentences you've created. Circle the **Center** and underline the **Head.** Now use just your green cards to begin ten more sentences. Finish 5 sentences with **pronouns** and 5 with **names** in the Center.

Why does the **adjective/descriptive** word come <u>first</u> in the Hawaiian sentence? Hawaiian was an oral language for thousands of years. Our kūpuna didn't get a "second glance" at the sentence; the first words they heard told them the most essential information. Don't forget that English word order is different from Hawaiian!

Homework 2-6

Matching. Write the number of the English sentence in front of the correct translation.

1. My mother is strong.	____ Māluhiluhi nō kēlā mahiʻai.
2. Aunty Lehua is little.	____ Hauʻoli ʻo Leināʻala.
3. The carpenter is really sad.	____ Maikaʻi ʻoe?
4. Leināʻala is happy.	____ Ikaika koʻu makuahine.
5. Your house is indeed old.	____ Kaumaha nō ke Kamana.
6. Is that student smart?	____ Liʻiliʻi ʻo ʻAnakē Lehua.
7. Her school is famous.	____ Maʻi nō wau.
8. That farmer is very tired.	____ Kahiko nō kou hale.
9. Are you well?	____ Kaulana kona kula.
10. I'm really sick.	____ Akamai kēlā haumāna?

Now divide the Hawaiian sentences into sections. Circle the **Center** subject and underline the **Head.**

Homework 2-7

What do these questions and answers mean? Circle the descriptive word. Draw a line between the Head and Center.

1. Kaulana ʻo Kahaʻi?
2. ʻAe, Kaulana ʻo ia.
3. Kaulana kona hoaaloha?
4. ʻAe, kaulana nō kona hoaaloha.

5. Maʻi koʻu makuakāne?
6. ʻAʻole. Māluhiluhi kou makuakāne.
7. Māluhiluhi ʻoe?
8. ʻAʻole. Maikaʻi au.

Homework 2-8

Translate the following into Hawaiian.

1, That store is old.
2. He is smart.
3. Her friend is nice.
4. My grandfather is big.
5. The farmer is famous.

6. This fisherman is hot.
7. Hilo is cold.
8. Nuʻumealani is tired.
9. I'm sick.
10. Your house is pretty!

Homework-2-9

Earlier we suggested using color-coded flashcards to learn your vocabulary. If **nouns** are orange, but **adjectives** are green, you can also use the flashcards to help you learn sentence patterns. Pick any green card **(adjective)** and place it in the **Head** position. Pick any orange card **(noun)** and place it in the **Center** position. Did you remember to include a **noun announcer** before the noun? What does your sentence say? Practice mixing vocabulary cards from several chapters to extend your list of possibilities.

d. Talking <u>to</u> someone and talking <u>about</u> someone: <u>e</u> and <u>'o</u>
Look back over the dialogs of this and the previous chapter to see how the words **e** and **'o** are used. What kinds of words does **e** come before? You know that **'o** is a **name announcer** and comes before **names,** usually people's names, but also before place names, names of stores, cars, houses, and so forth. Like **'o**, **e** is not translated into English, but is crucial to meaning in the Hawaiian sentence.

E is used to indicate that we are talking <u>**directly to**</u> someone. If I say **Aloha, e Kamalu** (Hello, Kamalu), I am talking to Kamalu. The **e** calls Kamalu's attention to the fact that I'm talking to him. If I say **E ke kauka, aloha ahiahi** (Doctor, good evening), again I'm talking directly to the doctor.

E can come before **noun announcer plus noun** combinations as well as before **names** and conveys the idea of "Hey, you, listen up. I'm talking to you." Remember that in addressing someone by his or her title (police officer, minister, teacher, father), we must use both **e** <u>and</u> the **noun announcer:**

E ka māka'i, pehea 'oe? (<u>Hey the</u> police officer, how are you?). In contrast, **'o** is used when we are talking <u>**about**</u> someone instead of talking to that person. When I ask **Pehea 'o Lokomaika'i?**, Lokomaika'i could be in the next room or in the Marquesas, since I'm **not** talking to him.

Self-Test 2-5

Fill in the blank using **e** or **'o**. Decide whether you are talking <u>to</u> or <u>about</u> the person. Then, translate into English.

_____ Leialoha, aloha awakea kāua!
Aloha kāua, _____ ke kaikamahine. Pehea _____ Nāinoa?
Māluhiluhi _____ Nāinoa, _____ Leialoha.

Auē! ____ ke kaikamahine, pehea 'oe?
Maika'i wau, ____ Leialoha. Pehea ____ Kalehua?
Ma'i ____ Kalehua, ____ ke kaikamahine.
A hui hou, __ Leialoha.
'Ae, aloha a hui hou, __ ke kaikamahine.

Homework 2-10

Draw a line from the Hawaiian to the correct translation.

1. E ke kumu, nāwaliwali 'o Keali'i?
2. 'Ae, e ke kaikamahine. Wela 'o Lahaina.
3. 'A'ole. Maika'i nō 'o Keali'i, e ke keiki.
4. Akamai 'o ia, e ko'u hoaaloha?
5. 'Ae. 'Eleu kēlā kāne, e ka wahine.
6. E Nāmau'u, pehea 'o Melelani?
7. Hau'oli ko'u* pōpoki, e Kau'i.
8. E ka lawai'a, 'ilihune 'o Uluwehi?

Yes, girl. Lahaina is hot.
Is he smart, my friend?
Namau'u, how is Melelani?
Fisherman, is Uluwehi poor?
Teacher, is Keali'i weak?
Yes, that man is lively, lady.
No. Keali'i is very well, boy.
My cat is happy, Kau'i.

Homework 2-11

Translate the following into Hawaiian.

1. How is Maui, Kainoa?
2. Maui is pretty, my friend.
3. Grandmother, is Leilehua sick?
4. Yes, Makana. Leilehua is sick.
5. No, Makana. Leilehua is well.

III. ORAL REVIEW AND PRACTICE - DRILLS, DIALOGS, STORIES

a. Substitution Drills

Kaumaha	**'o ia.**	kēia halekū'ai	**li'ili'i**
	'o Kaleialoha.		wela
	ke ali'i?		Hawai'i
	'oe.		'a'ala
	kona kupunakane		kaulana

Nani **ka wahine** nui.	**Wela** kou hoaaloha **akamai?**
'o Lahela	Ma'i nāwaliwali?
kona halekula	Pehea mālie?
ka mahi'ai	Hau'oli na'aupō?
kou makuahine	Ikaika Haole?
kēia hale	'Olu'olu 'āwīwī?

b. Practice with a Partner

Work the substitution drills in section **a** with a partner. Read the whole phrase to your partner. She will repeat after you. Tell your partner the underlined word; then say the first substitute word or words. She will repeat the entire phrase, replacing the underlined word with the substitute. Listen to the first Substitution Drill in Chapter 1 for an example. Switch off being the teacher and the student. Have your partner read phrases and sentences that you create with your flashcards. Translate. Turn some descriptive sentences into questions. How did you do that? Next add emphasis to the **Head.** What did you add?

Ask the following questions. Have your partner answer, choosing one of the clues provided. Repeat both question and answer; have your partner do the same. Listen to the examples on our CD.

1. Pehea kou makuakāne?   Maika'i nō ko'u makuakāne.
2. Hau'oli ke keiki ikaika?   'Ae, nui nō kona hale kahiko.
3. Pehea 'o Kaua'i?   'Ae, hau'oli ke keiki ikaika.
4. Nui kona hale kahiko?   'A'ole, kaumaha 'oia.
5. Pehea kēia halepule kaulana?   Mālie 'o Kaua'i.
                              'Olu'olu kēia halepule kaulana.
                              Pupuka kēia halepule kaulana.
                              'A'ole, li'ili'i kona hale.

Homework 2-12

Translate the following dialogs into Hawaiian.
Then, read your dialogs out loud by yourself or with a partner.

1. Good evening, lady.
   Good evening. How are you?
   I'm really tired. See you later.
   Yes, goodbye.

2. Hello to both of us, teacher.
Good morning, Ku'ulei.
How's the student?
She's fine, thanks.

3. Father (formal), hello.
Hello, Mokihana.
How's the store?
The store is fine.
Are you happy?
Yes, I'm really happy.

c. Picture Practice
1. Look at the pictures below. Make up a story to go along with the pictures.

What are the names of the people? How are they related? What do they say to each other?

2. We've made up a story about 'Ilima and her grandfather. Listen to the story on the CD several times as you read along. Now read the story aloud without listening to the CD. Listen to your pronunciation and phrasing. How smooth and fluent do you sound?

Kamaʻilio ʻo ʻIlima me kona kupunakāne.
ʻIlima: Pehea ʻoe, e koʻu kupunakāne?
Ke kupunakāne: Hauʻoli wau. A ʻo ʻoe, pehea ʻoe, e ʻIlima?
ʻIlima: Kaumaha ʻo Pāpā. Akā, maikaʻi nō wau.
Ke kupunakāne: Kaumaha ʻo Pāpā? He aha ka pilikia?
ʻIlima: ʻEha kona wāwae, e Tūtū. Maʻi ʻo ia.
Ke kupunakāne: Aloha nō!

ʻIlima talks with her grandfather.
ʻIlima: How are you, grandfather?
Grandfather: I'm happy. And you, how are you, ʻIlima?
ʻIlima: Daddy's sad. But I'm very well.
Grandfather: Daddy's sad? What's the problem?
ʻIlima: His leg is sore, Grandpa. He's sick.
Grandfather: Too bad!

d. Listen and Learn
Our new island is Kaua'i.

'O <u>Kaua'i</u> kēia mokupuni. 'O <u>Līhu'e</u> ke kūlanakauhale. He <u>poni</u> ka waiho'olu'u no <u>Kaua'i</u>. He lei <u>mokihana</u> kona lei. 'O <u>Manokalanipō</u> ke ali'i kaulana no Kaua'i. 'O Wai'ale'ale ke kuahiwi nani.

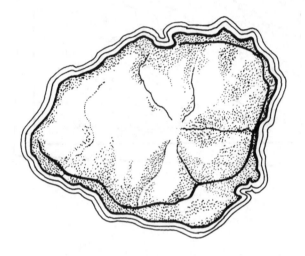

This island is <u>Kaua'i</u>. <u>Līhu'e</u> is the town. The color of <u>Kaua'i</u> is <u>purple.</u> Its lei is the <u>mokihana</u> lei. The famous chief of <u>Kaua'i</u> is <u>Manokalanipō</u>. The beautiful mountain is <u>Wai'ale'ale</u>.

Here is a slightly more difficult story provided largely as a listen- ing exercise. If you feel ready for a challenge, record yourself reading it and listen to the recording. How does your pronuncia- tion sound when compared with our version?

He mokupuni nani nō 'o Kaua'i. Kaulana nā pali o kēlā mokupuni kahiko. Nui nā po'e māka'ika'i e hahai ana i ke alahele mai Hā'ena mai a hiki i ke awāwa 'o Kalalau. Ua kapa 'ia kēia 'ao'ao o ka mokupuni 'o Nāpali, no ka nui o nā pali ki'eki'e o laila. 'O Hanakāpi'ai ke kahakai mua ma kēlā alahele. Ua 'ike paha 'oe i ka nani o Kaua'i, ka mokupuni "hemolele i ka mālie"?

Kaua'i is a very beautiful island. The cliffs of that old island are famous. Many tourists follow the trail from Hā'ena to Kalalau Valley. This side of the island is called Nāpali, because of the numerous tall

cliffs there. The first beach on this trail is Hanakāpī'ai. Have you per-
haps seen the beauty of Kaua'i, the island "pristine in calmness"?

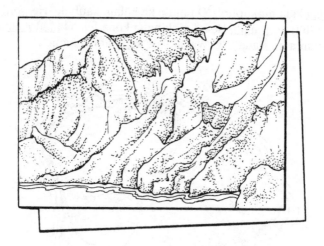

e. Mele

Learn the words to "Maika'i Kaua'i" and sing along with the CD.
This song mentions several places on Kaua'i, including its famous
mountain Wai'ale'ale; its lei, the mokihana; and the characterization
"Kaua'i hemolele i ka mālie," "Kaua'i pristine in calmness."

Maika'i Kaua'i (composer unknown)

Maika'i wale nō Kaua'i
Hemolele wale i ka mālie
Kuahiwi nani, Wai'ale'ale
Lei ana i ka mokihana.

Hui:
Maika'i nō Kaua'i
Hemolele i ka mālie
Kuahiwi Wai'ale'ale
Lei ana i ka mokihana.

Chapter Three

'O WAI IDENTIFICATION SENTENCE PATTERN: WHO ARE YOU?

I. ORAL WORK SECTION

a. Hakalama

Here is our second variation on the Hakalama chart, which is a duplication of the vowel. The repeated vowel requires an 'okina before it. Look for these words in the Hawaiian dictionary; how many of them have a meaning?

Haʻa Kaʻa Laʻa Maʻa Naʻa Paʻa Waʻa ʻAʻa
Heʻe Keʻe Leʻe Meʻe Neʻe Peʻe Weʻe ʻEʻe
Hiʻi Kiʻi Liʻi Miʻi Niʻi Piʻi Wiʻi ʻIʻi
Hoʻo Koʻo Loʻo Moʻo Noʻo Poʻo Woʻo ʻOʻo
Huʻu Kuʻu Luʻu Muʻu Nuʻu Puʻu Wuʻu ʻUʻu

Write out your own Hakalama variation chart with the kahakō. It should begin with Hāʻā Kāʻā Lāʻā and so forth. Next, read vertically down the lines of the chart above: say Haʻa Heʻe Hiʻi Hoʻo Huʻu. Read down each row; then do the same for the chart with the kahakō.

b. Vocabulary

Nouns		Adjectives	
ka **lawaiʻa**	fisherman	**lepo**	dirty
ka **iʻa**	fish	**maʻemaʻe**	clean
ka **mahiʻai**	farmer	**pōloli**	hungry
ka **māla**	garden	**māʻona**	full of food, satiated
ka **makuakāne**	father	**makewai**	thirsty
ka **makuahine**	mother	**kena**	not thirsty, quenched
ka **pua**	flower	**mōhala**	open (flower)
ka **lei**	garland	**mae**	wilted (flower)
ke **kumulāʻau**	tree	**lawa**	enough
ka **meakanu**	plant	**mākaukau**	prepared, ready
ke **kalo**	taro	**ʻono**	delicious
ka **maiʻa**	banana	**hāmama**	opened
ka **hana**	job, activity	**paʻa**	closed
ka **pāʻani**	game	**nīele**	nosy, inquisitive
ka **hula**	dance	**hemahema**	awkward, unskilled
ke **alakaʻi**	leader	**noʻeau**	clever, skilled
ke **mele**	song	**hewa**	wrong
ka **ʻuhane**	spirit	**pololei**	correct

c. Useful Phrases

E Kaipoleimanu.	(Hey) Kaipoleimanu.
E ke kāne.	(Hey) sir, gentleman.
E ka wahine.	(Hey) lady.
Auē!	Gosh! Wow! Too bad!
E kala mai.	Excuse me; I'm sorry.
E ʻoluʻolu.	Please.
Mahalo.	Thank you.
ʻAʻole pilikia.	No trouble/problem (you're welcome).**

ʻO wai kou inoa?	What's your name?
ʻO Kaleipua koʻu inoa.	Kaleipua is my name.

ʻO wai kona inoa?	What's his name?
ʻO Mamo kona inoa.	Mamo is his name.

ʻO wai ʻo ia?	Who is she?
ʻO Nohea ʻo ia.	She is Nohea.

ʻO wai kēlā aliʻi hanohano?
Who is that distinguished chief?

ʻO Kauikeaouli kēlā aliʻi hanohano.
That distinguished chief is Kauikeaouli.

Note that there is no Hawaiian equivalent for the English phrase "you're welcome" used in response to "thank you." **ʻAʻole pilikia means "no problem" and can be used for "you're welcome." You could also simply say "**mahalo**."

c. Dialogs

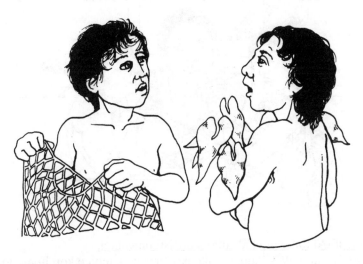

1. <u>Kama'ilio ka mahi'ai me ka lawai'a.</u>
Ka mahi'ai: 'O wai kou inoa?
Ka lawai'a: 'O Kaipoleimanu ko'u inoa.
Ka mahi'ai: 'Ō! 'O Kaipoleimanu kou inoa? 'O Nalu ko'u inoa.
Ka lawai'a: 'O wai ka inoa o kou makuakāne, e Nalu?
Ka mahi'ai: 'O La'akea ka inoa o ko'u makuakāne. 'O Kauhi ko'u inoa
    'ohana.
Ka lawai'a: Auē! 'O La'akea Kauhi kona inoa? Kama'āina au i kou
    makuakāne!

<u>The farmer talks with the fisherman.</u>
The farmer: What's your name?
The fisherman: My name is Kaipoleimanu.
The farmer: Oh! Your name is Kaipoleimanu? My name is Nalu.
The fisherman: What's the name of your father, Nalu?
The farmer: The name of my father is La'akea, My family name is Kauhi.
The fisherman: Wow! His name is La'akea Kauhi? I know your father!

2. <u>Kamaʻilio ʻo Kalei me Palakiko a me Nuʻumealani.</u>
Kalei: Aloha ʻauinalā kākou. E Palakiko, ʻo wai ka inoa o kou hoaaloha?
Palakiko: Aloha ʻauinalā, e Kalei. ʻO Nuʻumealani kēia.
Kalei: Hō! Nani kou inoa, e Nuʻumealani.
Nuʻumealani: Mahalo, e ka wahine. ʻO Kuʻulei kou inoa?
Kalei: ʻAʻole. ʻO Kalei koʻu inoa, e Nuʻumealani.
Nuʻumealani: Auē! E kala mai, e Kalei.
Kalei: ʻAʻole pilikia. Aloha a hui hou kākou!
Palakiko a me Nuʻumealani: A hui hou!

<u>Kalei speaks with Palakiko and Nuʻumealani.</u>
Kalei: Good afternoon everyone. Palakiko, what's the name of your
    friend?
Palakiko: Good afternoon, Kalei. This is Nuʻumealani.
Kalei: Wow! Your name is pretty, Nuʻumealani.
Nuʻumealani: Thanks, lady. Is your name Kuʻulei?
Kalei: No. My name is Kalei, Nuʻumealani.
Nuʻumealani: Gosh! Excuse me, Kalei.
Kalei: No problem. Goodbye 'til we all meet again!
Palakiko and Nuʻumealani: See you later!

II. GRAMMAR SECTION

a. 'O wai kou inoa: What's your name?

Greeting someone, saying aloha, is important in Hawaiian culture. If you do not first exchange greetings, you are not being polite. Again for politeness, you then ask how the person you've just greeted feels today. When meeting someone new, you should be polite and not ask his or her name until you have first greeted that person and asked how he or she is. Then you are ready to learn how to ask **what's your name?**

'O <u>wai</u> **kou** inoa?	What's **your** name?
'O <u>Kalei</u> **ko'u** inoa.	Kalei is **my** name.

What are the words that change in answering the question? First, notice that the question word **wai (who)** is simply replaced with the name in the answer. Second, the question asks for "**kou** inoa," "**your** name"; the answer responds with "**ko'u** inoa," "**my** name."

Although the **'O** is needed in both question and answer, it does not translate into English. The **'o** at the beginning of the sentence functions in Hawaiian just like a **name announcer** does; it gives the listener a clue that a name is coming and also emphasizes the name. Asking for the name of a person or place is translated by **'o wai** in Hawaiian; **wai** cannot stand alone. Unlike English, Hawaiian asks "<u>Who's</u> your name?" instead of "What's your name?"

Notice how similar the words for **your** and **my** are in Hawaiian. The word for **my** is **ko'u.** The word for **your** is **kou.** Alternate saying "my name," **ko'u inoa,** and "your name," **kou inoa,** <u>out loud</u> for a few minutes. Can you hear the extra syllable in **ko'u?** It's there because <u>I'm</u> special, so **I** get an extra sound (this may be helpful in distinguishing between **my** and **your,** but it is not a Hawaiian thought!).

Asking for the name of a third person is easier because the pronoun possessive **("kona," "his/her")** stays the same in both question and answer. **'O wai <u>kona</u> inoa? 'O <u>Mēlia</u> <u>kona</u> inoa.** All you have to do in the answer is substitute the person's name for the question word **wai.** Remember that **kona** means both **his** and **her.** Ko'u, kou and kona are noun announcers and may take the place of **ke/ka** or **kēia/kēlā** before nouns.

Self-Test 3-1

 Translate the following phrases.

1. your name
2. his house
3. her store
4. my name

5. my car
6. his name
7. your father
8. her church

9. your friend
10. her name
11. his mother
12. my husband

Homework 3-1

 Matching. Write the number of the Hawaiian sentence next to the correct English translation.

1. **'O wai kona inoa?**
2. **'O Niuli'i ko'u inoa.**
3. **'O wai ko'u inoa?**
4. **'O Keali'i ko'u inoa?**
5. **'O Makanani kou inoa.**
6. **'O wai kou inoa?**
7. **'O Wai'olu kona inoa.**
8. **'O Niuli'i kou inoa?**
9. **'O Heanu ko'u inoa.**
10. **'O Keali'i kou inoa.**

___ What's your name?
___ Makanani is your name.
___ Wai'olu is her name.
___ Niuli'i is my name.
___ What's her name?
___ Heanu is my name.
___ Keali'i is your name.
___ What is my name?
___ Is Keali'i my name?
___ Is Niuli'i your name?

Read the Hawaiian out loud. Which answers are appropriate responses to each question? There may be more than one appropriate response.

Homework 3-2

 Fill in the blank with the correct possessive pronoun.

What is her name?   **'O wai**_____**inoa?**
Her name is Lehua.   **'O Lehua**_____**inoa.**
What's your name?   **'O wai**_____**inoa?**
My name is Kāwika.   **'O Kāwika**_____**inoa.**
What's my name, mother?   **'O wai**_____**inoa, e ka makuahine?**
Your name is Keikilani.   **'O Keikilani**_____**inoa.**
Ku'ulei, what's his name? **E Ku'ulei, 'o wai**_____**inoa?**
His name is Nohea.   **'O Nohea**_____**inoa.**

Homework 3-3

Translate these questions and answers into Hawaiian.

1. What is his name?	His name is Kamanu.
2. What's your name?	My name is Melelani.
3. Melelani is your name.	Is your name Kamanu?
4. No, my name is Kawehiokekai.	Hello, Kawehiokekai.
5. Melelani, what's my name?	Your name is Nāmaka.
6. Is Nāmaka my name?	Yes, Nāmaka is my name.
7. What is her name, sir (man)?	Her name is Nani, lady.
8. Father, is your name Hauʻolimau?	No, my name is Hauʻolikeola.

b. ʻO Wai Pattern Variations: Changing the Center

In Chapter Two we found that our beginning-level sentence patterns will have only two sections, the <u>verb</u> or **Head** section and the <u>subject</u> or **Center** section.

Our question **ʻO wai kou inoa?** can be divided into two main sections:

HEAD: what/who	CENTER: subject
ʻO wai	kou inoa?

We can ask different **who** questions by changing the subject section of our sentence. How would you ask **Who's your friend?** Answer: ʻO wai **kou hoaaloha?** This subject substitution is our first variation on the basic **ʻO wai kou inoa** pattern.

We can place any kind of subject into the **Center** subject position, such as a pronoun, name announcer plus name, or noun announcer plus noun. If you answer the phone and want to know who's on the line, how would you say **Who is this?** Answer: ʻO wai **kēia? Kēia** and **kēlā** are the only noun announcers that can stand by themselves as subjects in some patterns.

HEAD	CENTER	
ʻO wai	kou inoa?	It is understood that the noun
ʻO wai	kou hoaaloha?	they announce in this usage is
ʻO wai	kēia?	**mea,** meaning **one, person,**
ʻO wai	ʻo ia?	**thing.** Therefore **ʻO wai kēia?** is
ʻO wai	**ʻo** Waiola?	understood to mean **ʻO wai kēia**
		mea? or **Who is this person?**

Self-Test 3-2

Translate the following into Hawaiian.

1. Who is that?   6. Who is this child?
2. Who is the teacher?   7. Who is Kāwika?
3. Who are you?   8. Who is my friend?
4. Who is that man?   9. Who is your father?
5. Who is she?   10. Who are we (all)?

III. ORAL REVIEW AND PRACTICE - DRILLS, DIALOGS, STORIES
a. Substitution Drills

ʻO wai **kēia makuahine?**   E **ke kauka,** aloha ʻauinalā!
         kona kaʻa?   Healani
         ka halekūʻai?   ka lawaiʻa
         kou hoahānau?   ke kāpena
         kēlā mokupuni?   Kahulu
         koʻu* pōpoki?   ka papa

Puamēlia, ʻo **wai** kou hoaaloha?   O wai **ʻo Keʻeaumoku?**
          koʻu* keiki   Maile   kēia?
          ka makuakāne   kēlā   kona kupunawahine?
          Līhau   wau   ʻo ia?
          ke kāpena   Keawe   ke kauka?
          Alona   kēia wahine   ʻo Nāihe?

For an extra challenge, listen to the CD without looking at the book. Do you understand everything? Can you transcribe what you hear?

b. Picture Practice

1. Look at the picture below. Make up a story to go along with the picture. What are the names of the people? How are they related? What do they say to each other?

2. We have made up a story about two friends eating lunch near the university.

Ke kama'ilio nei 'o Līhau me kona hoaaloha. 'O Nai'a ka inoa o kona hoaaloha. Aia 'o Līhau a me Nai'a i ka hale 'aina. Kokoke kēia hale 'aina i ke kula nui. Nui nā haumāna e hele mai ana no ka 'aina awakea.

Līhau: E Nai'a, 'o wai ka inoa o kēlā wahine? He haumāna 'o ia ma ke
     kula nui? Kama'āina 'oe iā ia?
Nai'a: 'Ae. 'O Mamo kona inoa. 'O ko'u hoaaloha 'o ia. E Mamo, aloha
     awakea!
Mamo: Aloha nō, e Nai'a. 'O wai ka inoa o kou hoaaloha?
Nai'a: 'O Līhau kēia. E Līhau, 'o ko'u hoaaloha kēia. 'O Mamo kona inoa.
Līhau: Aloha, e Mamo. Pehea 'oe i kēia awakea?
Mamo: Māluhiluhi au, e Līhau. Nui ka hana ma ke kula.
Līhau: 'Ae, pololei 'oe. Nui ka hana.

Līhau is talking with her friend. Her friend's name is Nai'a. Līhau and Nai'a are at a restaurant. This restaurant is close to the university. There are lots of students coming in for lunch.

Līhau: Nai'a, what's the name of that woman? Is she a student at the
    university? Do you know her?
Nai'a: Yes. Her name is Mamo. She's my friend. Mamo, good noontime!
Mamo: Hello indeed, Nai'a. What's the name of your friend?
Nai'a: This is Līhau. Līhau, this is my friend. Her name is Mamo.
Līhau: Hello, Mamo. How are you this noon?
Mamo: I'm tired, Līhau. There's a lot of work at school.
Līhau: Yes, you're right. Lots of work.

c. Listen and Learn

Our new island is O'ahu.

'O <u>O'ahu</u> kēia mokupuni. 'O <u>Honolulu</u> ke kūlanakauhale. He <u>melemele</u>
ka waiho'olu'u no <u>O'ahu.</u> He lei <u>'ilima</u> kona lei. 'O <u>Kākuhihewa</u> ke ali'i
kaulana no <u>O'ahu</u>. 'O <u>Ka'ala</u> ke kuahiwi nani.

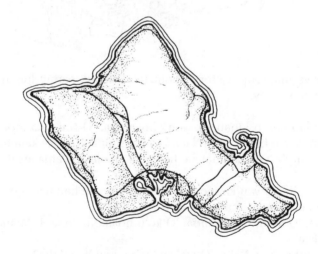

This island is <u>O'ahu</u>. <u>Honolulu</u> is the town. The color of <u>O'ahu</u> is <u>yel-
low</u>. Its lei is the <u>'ilima</u> lei. The famous chief of <u>O'ahu</u> is <u>Kākuhihewa</u>.
The beautiful mountain is Ka'ala.

Do you remember the names in the story for Niʻihau? for Kauaʻi? See if you can fill in the blanks without looking back at the previous chapters.

ʻO <u>Niʻihau</u> kēia mokupuni. ʻO _____ ke kūlanakauhale. He ka waihoʻoluʻu no_____. He lei_____kona lei. ʻO_____ke aliʻi kaulana no_____. ʻO_____ke kuahiwi nani.

ʻO <u>Kauaʻi</u> kēia mokupuni. ʻO_____ke kūlanakauhale. He_____ ka waihoʻoluʻu no_____. He lei_____kona lei. ʻO_____ke aliʻi kaulana no_____. ʻO_____ke kuahiwi nani.

As a further listening challenge, we offer a more difficult story about Oʻahu island.

Nui ka poʻe e noho ana ma ka mokupuni ʻo Oʻahu. Aia ke kapikala o kēia paeʻāina ma laila. Noho ke kiaʻāina ma Honolulu. ʻO John Waiheʻe ka inoa o ke kiaʻāina. He Hawaiʻi ʻo ia. Noho ʻo Waiheʻe ma ka hale ʻo Washington Place. Kokoke ʻo Washington Place i ka hale aliʻi ʻo ʻIolani. He kūlanakauhale nui ʻo Honolulu a nui nā kaʻa e holo wikiwiki ana ma ʻō a ma ʻaneʻi. Nui nō hoʻi ka poʻe mākaʻikaʻi mai nā ʻāina ʻē mai e kipa mai ana i nā hōkele ma Waikīkī.

There are lots of people living on the island of Oʻahu. The capital of this island chain is there. The governor lives in Honolulu. The name of the governor is John Waiheʻe. He's a Hawaiian. Waiheʻe lives in a house named Washington Place. Washington Place is near 'Iolani Palace. Honolulu is a large city and there are lots of cars going quickly here and there. There are also lots of tourists from foreign lands visiting the hotels in Waikīkī.

d. Mele

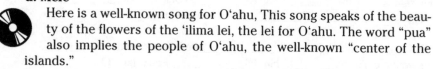

Here is a well-known song for O'ahu, This song speaks of the beauty of the flowers of the 'ilima lei, the lei for O'ahu. The word "pua" also implies the people of O'ahu, the well-known "center of the islands."

Nā Pua ka 'Ilima, by Kau'i Zuttermeister

Nani wale nā pua lei ka 'ilima
'O ka u'i ho'oheno o Kākuhihewa

Kūlana hiehie me ka hanohano
Ha'aheo i ka maka ke 'ike aku

Ho'ohihi ka mana'o i laila
Nā pua lei 'ilima e kaulana nei

Kaulana nā pua lei ka 'ilima
Ke kikowaena o nā 'ailana

'Ohu'ohu wale a i nā malihini
Ka nani kaulana poina 'ole

Ha'ina 'ia mai ana ka puana
Nā pua lei 'ilima e kaulana nei

Chapter Four

HE AHA SENTENCE AND IDENTIFICATION PATTERN: WHAT'S THIS?

I. ORAL WORK SECTION

a. Hakalama

Here is another variation of the Hakalama chart; as in Chapter Three, we are adding a second vowel to the basic syllable, but now we change the second vowel.

> Haʻe Kaʻe Laʻe Maʻe Naʻe Paʻe Waʻe ʻAʻe
> Heʻa Keʻa Leʻa Meʻa Neʻa Peʻa Weʻa ʻEʻa
> Hiʻe Kiʻe Liʻe Miʻe Niʻe Piʻe Wiʻe ʻIʻe
> Hoʻa Koʻa Loʻa Moʻa Noʻa Poʻa Woʻa ʻOʻa
> Huʻe Kuʻe Luʻe Muʻe Nuʻe Puʻe Wuʻe ʻUʻe

Read down each column: **Haʻe Heʻa Hiʻe Hoʻa Huʻe**. Read each line from right to left: **ʻAʻe Waʻe Paʻe Naʻe Maʻe** and so forth. Make up your own chart with kahakō variations: **Haʻē Kaʻē Laʻē Maʻē** or **Hāʻe Kāʻe Lāʻe Māʻe**. Weʻve added only the letters **e** or **a** as the second letters in each line. Make up your own Hakalama variation by substituting **i, o** or **u: Hoʻi Koʻi Loʻi**. What comes next?

b. Vocabulary

Nouns		Adjectives	
ke **kinai ahi**	firefighter	**waiwai**	valuable, wealthy
ke **kauka**	doctor	**ʻilihune**	poor
ka **haukapila**	hospital	**hilahila**	embarrassed, ashamed
ke **keikikāne**	son, boy	**haʻaheo**	proud
ke **kaikamahine**	daughter, girl	**pono**	righteous
ke **kino**	body	**kūpono**	appropriate, proper
ka **puʻuwai**	heart	**uʻi**	beautiful (people)
ke **poʻo**	head	**paʻakikī**	difficult, hard
ka **maka**	eye, face	**maʻalahi**	easy
ka **lima**	hand, arm	**pipiʻi**	expensive
ka **wāwae**	foot, leg	**emi**	cheap
ke **kua**	back	**ʻeleu**	lively
ka **waha**	mouth	**moloā**	lazy
ka **ʻōpū**	stomach	**kolohe**	mischievous
ka **lole**	clothes	**kāpulu**	messy
ka **pāpale**	hat	**haʻahaʻa**	low, humble

ke **kāma'a**   shoe   **ki'eki'e**   high up, tall
ka **makaaniani**   eyeglasses
ka **uaki**   watch, clock

c. Useful Phrases

He aha kēia?	What's this?
He pua kēia.	This is a flower.

He pua 'a'ala kēlā?	Is that a fragrant flower?
'Ae. He pua 'a'ala kēlā.	Yes, that is a fragrant flower.

He 'ohana lākou?	Are they a family?
'A'ole. He hālau hula lākou.	No. They are a hula troupe.

He kinai ahi pono 'o Keahi?	Is Keahi a righteous fireman?
'Ae. He kinai ahi pono 'o ia.	Yes, he is a righteous fireman.

He Hawai'i ha'aheo au.	I am a proud Hawaiian.

Maopopo iā 'oe?	Do you understand?
'Ae, maopopo ia'u.	Yes, I understand.
'A'ole maopopo ia'u.	I don't understand.

The colors listed below are adjectives and should be on green flash-cards.

'ele'ele	black	**ke'oke'o**	white
'ula'ula	red	**'alani**	orange
melemele	yellow	**'ōma'oma'o**	green
uliuli	blue	**poni**	purple
'ākala	pink	**hinahina**	grey

d. Dialogs

1. <u>Kamaʻilio ʻo Kealiʻi me ke keikikāne.</u>
Ke keikikāne: E Kealiʻi, he aha kēlā?
Kealiʻi: He pāpale hou kēlā.
Ke keikikāne: He pāpale emi kēlā?
Kealiʻi; ʻAʻole. Pipiʻi koʻu pāpale hou.
Ke keikikāne: He pāpale lauhala kou pāpale hou?
Kealiʻi: ʻAe, pololei. He hana noʻeau Hawaiʻi ka ulana lauhala.

<u>Kealiʻi talks with the boy.</u>
Boy: Kealiʻi, what's that?
Kealiʻi: That's a new hat.
Boy: Is that an inexpensive hat?
Kealiʻi: No. My new hat is expensive.
Boy: Is your new hat a lauhala hat?
Kealiʻi: Yes, that's right. Weaving lauhala is a Hawaiian craft.

2. <u>Kamaʻilio ʻo Kuʻuwehi me kona hoaaloha hou.</u>
Kona hoaaloha: He aha kou makuahine?
Kuʻuwehi: He Hawaiʻi koʻu makuahine.
Kona hoaaloha: ʻAʻole kēlā ka nīnau. He aha kona* hana?
Kuʻuwehi: E kala mai. He kinai ahi koʻu makuahine.
Kona hoaaloha: He kanaka ikaika kou makuahine?
Kuʻuwehi: ʻŌ! ʻAe. He kinai ahi ikaika koʻu makuahine.

<u>The woman talks with her new friend.</u>
Her friend: What's your mother?
Kuʻuwehi: My mother's a Hawaiian.
Her friend: That's not the question. What's her job?
Kuʻuwehi: Excuse me. My mother is a firefighter.
Her friend: Is your mother a strong person?
Kuʻuwehi: Oh! Yes. My mother is a strong firefighter.

II. GRAMMAR SECTION

a. He aha kēia?
Our new sentence pattern is a most useful one since it asks **What is
this?** In the **He aha kēia** pattern, the question word **aha** is replaced
with the answer. He **aha kēia?** asks for a <u>common noun</u> as the answer.

He <u>aha</u> kēia?   <u>What</u> is this?

He <u>pōpoki</u> kēia.   This is a <u>cat.</u>

Look once more at the question in Hawaiian and English. **Aha** means **what**. **He** means **a/an**. There is no verb "to be" in Hawaiian. Therefore you are literally asking **a what this?** and your answer will always have **a** or **an** in the English translation.

In light of your understanding of Hawaiian word order and the parts of a simple Hawaiian sentence, can you decide which is the **Center** of the **He aha kēia** question? Did you choose **kēia**? **Maika'i!** We look for the **Center** first, since that is the subject or focus of the sentence. What is the **Head** section of this sentence?

Head: A what   **Center:** this
He aha   **kēia?**

Self-Test 4-1

Using nouns from your vocabulary lists, make up questions and answers that identify the pictures below. Follow our example. E.g., picture of lei - He aha kēia? - He lei kēia.

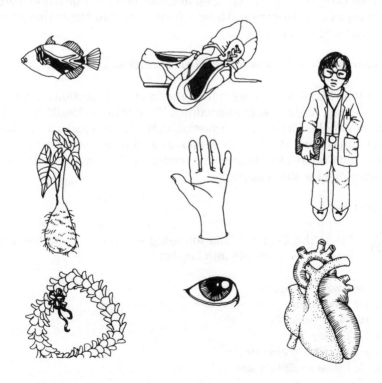

It is obvious that this new question pattern is an excellent one for learning new nouns in your vocabulary. There are also different kinds of questions we can ask with the **He aha** pattern, as we change the **Center**. What are the different kinds of **Center** subjects we've learned? How would we ask "What's <u>that</u>?"

HEAD: A what	**CENTER:**
He aha	**kēlā?**
He aha	ka māka'i?
He aha	'o ia?
He aha	**'o** Makanani?

Self-Test 4-2

Make up two **He aha** questions for each of the different types of Center subjects: pronouns, noun announcer plus noun, name announcer plus name, **kēia/kēlā.**

b. He plus noun pattern
You now know that in answering **he aha** questions, the question word **aha** is replaced with a noun. These answers are statements that identify something or someone.

He kahunapule kēia makuahine. This mother is a minister.

Divide the Hawaiian sentence into Center and Head sections. What is in the Center? Answer: **kēia makuahine.** What is in the Head? Answer: **He kahunapule.** The extra information in the Head tells us about the Center subject: we identify this person as a minister. Now we can create **He plus noun** identification sentences in the same way that we answered the **He aha** questions.

Self-Test 4-3

 Circle the Center in the following sentences. Underline the Head. Then translate into English.

1. He lawai'a ke kāpena.
2. He Hawai'i au.
3. He i'a ka mahimahi.
4. He malihini 'oe.
5. He haumāna 'o Noenoe.
6. He haleleka kēlā hale nui?

7. He kupunakāne kēia mākaʻi.
8. He ʻohana nui lākou.
9. He ʻāina ua ʻo Mānoa?
10. He makuahine ʻo ia?

The pattern for our new **He plus noun** sentence is to have **he** plus a common noun in the **Head** section and the regular subject variations (name announcer plus name, noun announcer plus noun, pronouns, kēia/kēlā) in the **Center** section. **He** is a noun announcer; no other noun announcer is needed in the **Head**.

HEAD: **He plus noun**	CENTER:
He hale ʻaina	**kēia hale.**
This building is a restaurant.	
He mokupuni	**ʻo Nihoa.**
Nihoa is an island.	
He wilikī	**ʻoe?**
Are you an engineer?	
He mahiʻai	**kou* moʻopunakāne?**
Is your grandson a farmer?	

The correspondence between **he** and **a/an** is a big help in recognizing when to use a **he plus noun** pattern. The English gives us a giant clue: any English sentence with **a** or **an** following the verb **to be** (. . . **is a** . . .), (. . . **are an** . . .) must be translated with the **He** plus <u>common noun</u> pattern.

Questions and statements are sometimes distinguished from each other only through intonation. Listen to the different ways these statements and questions are said.

This is **a** <u>fisherman.</u>	**He** <u>lawaiʻa</u> kēia.
Is this **a** <u>fisherman?</u>	**He** <u>lawaiʻa</u> kēia?
That bird is **an** <u>owl.</u>	**He** <u>pueo</u> kēlā manu.
Is that bird **an** <u>owl?</u>	**He** <u>pueo</u> kēlā manu?
Is your father **a** <u>captain?</u>	**He** <u>kāpena</u> kou makuakāne?
Your father is **a** <u>captain.</u>	**He** <u>kāpena</u> kou makuakāne.

Note that in asking questions with the **he plus noun** pattern there is no change in the Hawaiian sentence except for punctuation.

Self-Test 4-4

Pick ten nouns from your vocabulary flashcards. Make up five **he plus noun** sentences to say out loud. Use one noun in the Center and one in the Head for each sentence.

Self-Test 4-5

Test a partner: Hold up any two noun cards and have your partner create as many different **He aha** questions as she can using these two nouns. Have her answer the questions.

Homework 4-1

Matching. Write the number of the Hawaiian sentence next to its English translation.

1. He aha kou* lawai'a?   Her friend is a Japanese.
2. He Pukikī 'o ia.   My dog is a spaniel.
3. He kupuna kēia kāne.   What is this person?
4. He spaniel ko'u* 'īlio.   What is that teacher?
5. He Kepanī kona hoaaloha.   He's a Portuguese.
6. He kinai ahi ko'u makuakāne. What is your fisherman?
7. He aha kēlā kumu?   That teacher is a farmer.
8. He aha kēia kanaka?   The building is a hospital.
9. He mahi'ai kēlā kumu.   My father is a firefighter.
10. He haukapila ka hale.   This man is a grandparent.

Homework 4-2

Translate the following sentences into Hawaiian.

1. What is her friend?
2. Her friend is a Hawaiian. (**Hawai'i**)
3. What is the homework?
4. A book is the homework.
5. What is this commoner?
6. This commoner is a farmer.
7. What is the police officer?
8. The police officer is a grandmother.

9. What is your baby?
10. My baby is a boy.

c. Translation Tricks

Here are some tricks for translating from English sentences into Hawaiian; these tricks will work for the **he aha** as well as **descriptive** and other simple Hawaiian sentence patterns. They will <u>not</u> work for most questions, since questions usually have their own special patterns. Using nouns from your vocabulary lists, write out five English sentences following this pattern:

<u>Subject</u>   **is a/an** <u>noun.</u>
This doctor   **is a** woman.

Next, write out **<u>Head</u>** and **<u>Center</u>** headings for the Hawaiian sentence sections. Cross out the verb **is (am, are, was, were).** Circle any words that come before the verb in the English sentence and write them under the <u>Center</u> heading. Do not translate yet.

Head   **Center**
                                      this doctor

Go back to the English sentence and cross out those words. What's left to translate? **a woman**. Place this phrase under the <u>Head</u> heading. Do not translate it yet.

Head   **Center**
A woman   this doctor.

Look at the Head section: What clue does it give you as to the correct Hawaiian pattern for this sentence? It tells you to start the Hawaiian sentence with **He.** Go ahead and translate.

This doctor is a woman.
    <u>Head</u>   **<u>Center</u>**
    A woman   this doctor.
    He wahine   **kēia kauka.**

Self-Test 4-6

Using different noun flashcards, make up several more **He plus noun** sentences to say out loud. Translate into English.

III. ORAL REVIEW AND PRACTICE - DRILLS, DIALOGS, STORIES

a. Substitution Drills

He **haumāna** 'o Ke'alohi.	He **kinai ahi**	**ko'u hoahānau.**
Kepanī	lawai'a	wau.
kupunakāne	mahi'ai	kēlā makuahine.
inoa	kupunawahine	'o Nāmanu.
aha ?	kahunapule	ke kāne.
kanaka	pua'a	'o ia

He **aha**	**kou*** hana?	He **puke**	**Hawai'i**	**Kona*** puke?
ha'awina	kēia pepa?	Ford	kahiko	kona kalaka?
mokupuni	'o Kaho'olawe.	kalakoa	kolohe	ka pōpoki
mau ali'i	kākou.	lei po'o	'a'ala	kēia lei?
mea kanu	ka maile.	nai'a	'eleu	kēlā i'a?

b. Picture Practice

1. Look at the picture below. Make up a story to go along with the picture. What are the names of the people? How are they related? What do they say to each other?

2. We have made up a story about Kemomi and her tūtū, who are picking limu at the beach.

Aia ʻo Kemomi a me kona kupunawahine i kahakai. Ke ʻohi nei ʻo tūtū i ka limu. Kōkua ʻo Kemomi.

Kemomi: E Tūtū, he aha kēia? He limu kēia?
Tūtū: He limu kēia, e Kemomi. ʻAʻole naʻe kēia he limu maikaʻi.
Kemomi: He aha ka limu maikaʻi?
Tūtū: He limu maikaʻi ka limu Wāwaeʻiole.
Kemomi: He aha ke ʻano o ka limu Wāwaeʻiole, e Tūtū?
Tūtū: Mānoanoa ka limu Wāwaeʻiole. E nānā mai i kēia Wāwaeʻiole. Ua like ka limu me ka wāwae o ka ʻiole.
Kemomi: Auē! Ua akamai ka poʻe kahiko. He inoa maikaʻi kēlā.

Kemomi and her grandmother are at the beach. Tūtū is gathering seaweed. Kemomi helps.

Kemomi: Tūtū, what is this? Is this seaweed?
Tūtū: This is seaweed, Kemomi. However, it's not a good seaweed.
Kemomi: What is good seaweed?
Tūtū: Wāwaeʻiole (rat's foot) seaweed is a good seaweed.
Kemomi: What kind of seaweed is the Wāwaeʻiole, Tūtū?
Tūtū: Wāwaeʻiole seaweed is thick. Look at this Wāwaeʻiole. The seaweed is like the foot of the rat.
Kemomi: Wow! The people of old were clever! That's a good name.

c. Listen and Learn

Our new island is Moloka'i.

'O <u>Moloka'i</u> kēia mokupuni. 'O <u>Kaunakakai</u> ke kūlanakauhale. He <u>'ōma'oma'o</u> ka waiho'olu'u no <u>Moloka'i.</u> He lei <u>kukui</u> kona lei. 'O <u>Lanikāula</u> ke ali'i kaulana no <u>Moloka'i.</u> 'O Kamakou ke kuahiwi nani.

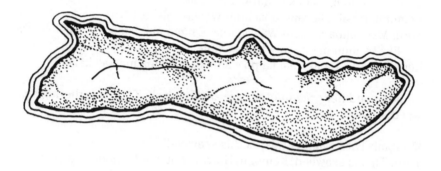

This island is <u>Moloka'i.</u> <u>Kaunakakai</u> is the town. The color of <u>Moloka'i</u> is <u>green.</u> Its lei is the <u>kukui</u> lei. The famous chief of <u>Moloka'i</u> is <u>Lanikāula</u>. The beautiful mountain is <u>Kamakou</u>.

Can you remember the names, color and lei for O'ahu? Fill in the blanks; then read your story out loud. If you've forgotten any answers, instead of looking back to Chapter Three, find the O'ahu story on the CD. Try to write down the Hawaiian words from <u>listening</u> only.

'O <u>O'ahu</u> kēia mokupuni. 'O_____ke kūlanakauhale. He_____ ka waiho'olu'u no_____ He lei_____kona lei. 'O_____ke ali'i kaulana no_____. 'O_____ke kuahiwi nani.

As a further listening challenge, we offer a more difficult story about Moloka'i. Listen along with the CD.

Ua kaulana ka mokupuni li'ili'i 'o Moloka'i i ka wā kahiko i ka mana. I ka wā kaua, ua kia'i 'ia 'o Moloka'i e nā kāhuna, 'a'ole e nā koa. Ua ikaika ka pule a nā kāhuna e like me Lanikāula. He 'ano kahuna 'o Lanikāula; he kahuna wānana 'o ia. Aia kona ulu kukui ma Kalama'ula. He hō'ailona ke kukui no ka na'auao. Ua nui ka na'auao a me ka mana o nā kāhuna o Moloka'i. Ua 'ōlelo 'ia kekahi 'ōlelo no'eau e pili ana iā Moloka'i, 'o ia ho'i, 'o "Moloka'i pule o'o."

The little island of Moloka'i was well known in the olden days for spiritual power. In times of war, Moloka'i was guarded by the kahuna, not by soldiers. The prayers of kahuna like Lanikāula were strong. Lanikāula was a kind of kahuna; he was a prophet. His kukui grove is at Kalama'ula. The kukui is a symbol of wisdom. Great was the wisdom and spiritual power of the kahuna of Moloka'i. A wise saying is said about Moloka'i, that is, "Moloka'i of the mature prayer."

d. Mele

Here is a well-known song for Moloka'i. Listen to the CD and sing along.

This song tells the love of a Moloka'i native for the waterfalls whose spray adorns the cliffs of his birthplace.

Moloka'i Waltz, by Matthew Kane

He nani kū kilakila
alo lua i nā pali
home aloha nō ia
ku'u one hānau
wailele hune nā pali
kou kāhiko nō ia
me Moloka'i 'āina kaulana
me 'oe nō au.

Chapter Five

ACTION SENTENCES: VERBS AT LAST!

I. ORAL WORK SECTION

a. Hakalama Here is our fourth variation on the Hakalama chart, which is a diphthong, or a combination of two vowels whose sounds blend together. This is our most challenging Hakalama chart so far! Be sure to pronounce the first vowel clearly before you blend it into the second. Repeated practice will make this new Hakalama variation easier on your mouth muscles.

Hae	Hai	Hao	Hau
Kae	Kai	Kao	Kau
Lae	Lai	Lao	Lau
Mae	Mai	Mao	Mau
Nae	Nai	Nao	Nau
Pae	Pai	Pao	Pau
Wae	Wai	Wao	Wau

b. Vocabulary

Make flashcards to help yourself learn the words. Use a **new** color index card for **verbs:** we've chosen to use <u>yellow</u>.

Nouns		Verbs	
ke **kama'āina**	local person	**hele mai**	to come
ka **malihini**	newcomer, guest	**hele**	to go
ka **'aumakua**	guardian spirit	**hana**	to work
ka **mo'opunakāne**	grandson	**pā'ani**	to play
ka **mo'opunawahine**	granddaughter	**nīnau**	to question
ka **hō'ike**	show, display	**pane**	to answer
ke **kelepona**	telephone	**'ai**	to eat
ka **makana**	gift	**inu**	to drink
ka **lā hānau**	birthday	**'ōlelo**	to speak
ka **pā'ina**	party	**hō'ike**	to show
ke **kālā**	money	**noho**	to sit, stay someplace
ke **kumukū'ai**	price	**kū**	to stand
ka **halekū'ai**	store	**alaka'i**	to lead
ke **kikowaenakū'ai**	shopping center	**māka'ika'i**	to sightsee
ka **hōkele**	hotel	**'ike**	to see
ka **lumi**	room	**hā'awi**	to give
ke **kahakai**	beach	**kū'ai mai**	to buy
ke **one**	sand	**kū'ai aku**	to sell

c. Useful Phrases

i ka halekū'ai pipi'i	at the expensive store
i ke kikowaenakū'ai 'o Ala Moana	at Ala Moana shopping center
i kona kula	at his school, in his school
i ka hōkele kaulana	at the famous hotel, in the famous hotel

'Ōlelo kona kupunawahine.
Her grandmother speaks.

'Ōlelo kona kupunawahine i ka 'ōlelo Hawai'i.
Her grandmother speaks Hawaiian.

Kū'ai mai 'o Lei i ka makana.
Lei buys the gift.

Kū'ai mai 'o Lei i ka makana i ke kikowaenakū'ai 'o Ala Moana.
Lei buys the gift at Ala Moana shopping center.

Pā'ani ka malihini.
The newcomer plays.

Pā'ani ka malihini i ke one.
The newcomer plays in the sand.

d. Dialogs

1. <u>Kamaʻilio ʻo Kōnane me Nohea.</u>
Kōnane: Aloha ahiahi, e Nohea. Hana ʻoe i kēia halekūʻai?
Nohea: Aloha, e Kōnane. ʻAe, hana wau i ke kikowaenakūʻai ʻo Ala
  Moana. Hele mai ka poʻe mākaʻikaʻi i kēia halekūʻai. Kūʻai lākou i ka
  muʻumuʻu a me ka pālule aloha.
Kōnane: ʻAe. He halekūʻai kaulana kēia. Ua lawe mai wau i koʻu
  malihini. Ke kūʻai mai nei ʻo ia i ka muʻumuʻu hou.
Nohea: Maikaʻi. He kūʻaiemi kēia.

<u>Kōnane talks with Nohea.</u>
Kōnane: Good evening, Nohea. Do you work in this store?
Nohea: Hello, Kōnane. Yes, I work at Ala Moana shopping center.
  Tourists come to this store. They buy muʻumuʻus and aloha shirts.
Kōnane. Yes. This is a famous store. I brought my guest. She's buying
a new muʻumuʻu.
Nohea: Good. This is a sale.

2. <u>Kamaʻilio ke kamaʻāina me kona hoahānau.</u>
Ke kamaʻāina: Ke noho nei ʻoe i kēia hōkele nani?
Kona hoahānau: ʻAʻole. Ua hele mai au i ka pāʻina lā hānau.
Ke kamaʻāina: E ʻike ana ʻoukou i ka hōʻike hula?
Kona hoahānau: ʻAe. Hula kou makuakāne i ka hōʻike hula?
Ke kamaʻāina: ʻAe. Alakaʻi koʻu makuakāne i kēlā hōʻike.
Kona hoahānau: Maikaʻi. E hāʻawi ana au i kēia lei maile i kou
  makuakāne.

The local person talks with his cousin.
Local person: Are you staying at this pretty hotel?
His cousin: No. I came to a birthday party.
Local person: Are you all going to see the hula show?
His cousin: Yes. Does your father dance in the hula show?
Local person: Yes. My father leads that hula show.
His cousin: Good. I will give this maile lei to your father.

II. GRAMMAR SECTION

a. Adding Verbs to Our Sentence: Action in the Head!

The **Head** section of Hawaiian sentences can hold any number of different sentence pattern beginnings. It is the **Head** section that tells us **what kind** of pattern our sentence is. In this chapter we are adding action to the **Head** by introducing action verbs. The simplest verb pattern conveys the idea of a habitual action, something that you do often, on an ongoing basis.

Nānā ke kāne.	The man looks.
Hana ʻoe.	You work.
Heluhelu kou* kāpena.	Your captain reads.
ʻAi ʻo Kanoe.	Kanoe eats.
ʻŌlelo ke aliʻi.	The chief speaks.
Hui kākou.	We all meet.

Self-Test 5-1

Circle the **Centers** of these simple sentences and underline the **Heads.**
Next, color the **Centers** orange and the **Heads** yellow.

Head: **verb**	Center:
Nānā	ke kāne.
Hana	ʻoe.
Heluhelu	kou* kāpena.
ʻAi	ʻo Kanoe.
ʻŌlelo	ke aliʻi.
Hui	kākou.

Homework 5-1

Pick any yellow **verb** flashcard and form a sentence by adding
it to the Centers below. Try several verbs with each Center.
Translate your sentences.

    1. . . . 'o Leialoha
    2. . . . ke kumu
    3. . . . 'o ia
    4. . . . kona* keiki
    5. . . . ka wahine

Homework 5-2

Make up sentences with your vocabulary verbs. Start by picking up a
yellow **verb** flashcard. Add the usual Center variations.

Homework 5-3

Translate the following into Hawaiian.

  1. This doctor works.
  2. Ku'upuni asks.
  3. I go.
  4. The student answers.
  5. That chief leads.

  6. We all eat.
  7. Her minister sits.
  8. This fisherman sees.
  9. Nāinoa plays.
 10. You speak the Hawaiian language.

b. Hawaiian Verb Markers: Adding Time to the Action

Tense markers do not make our sentence uptight; they allow us to time
our actions! Past, present and future actions in Hawaiian sentences are
indicated by words we add to the Head, before and after the **verb.**

Hana 'oe.	You work.
Ua hana 'oe.	You wor<u>ked</u>.
Ke hana **nei** 'oe.	You <u>are working</u>.
E hana **ana** 'oe.	You <u>will work.</u>

How do English verbs change to indicate tense? Unlike Hawaiian verbs,
English verbs usually change their <u>form</u> to show past, present or
future. Hawaiian verbs add verb markers instead of changing their
form. What is the Hawaiian verb marker for the past time action? For
present? for future?

Ua Verb	=	**past** action. It's over now.
Ke Verb **nei**	=	**present** action. It's going on now.
E Verb **ana**	=	**future** action. It will happen later.

Remember that it is not necessary to have any tense markers in the Head; the verb can stand by itself. A "naked" verb is timeless. That is, it indicates an ongoing, habitual action, something you do regularly.

Hana au i ka hale. I work at home.
Nānā kēia keiki i ke kīwī. This child watches TV.

Now change these sentences to "I work<u>ed</u> at home" and "This child watch<u>ed</u> TV." What did you add to your timeless sentence? Where? Your new sentences should be <u>**Ua**</u> **hana au i ka hale** and <u>**Ua**</u> **nānā kēia keiki i ke kīwī.** Next change these sentences to "I <u>will</u> work at home" and "This child <u>will</u> watch TV." How did you change your past tense sentence? Your new sentences should be <u>**E**</u> **hana** <u>**ana**</u> **au i ka hale** and <u>**E**</u> **nānā** <u>**ana**</u> **kēia keiki i ke kīwī.**

Homework 5-4

 Matching. Write the number of the Hawaiian sentence next to its English translation.

1. Ua mākaʻikai ʻo Kanalu i kēia kakahiaka.
2. E nīnau ana lākou i ka mākaʻi.
3. Ke noho nei koʻu* ʻīlio i koʻu kaʻa.
4. Kūʻai aku kēlā kāne i ka ʻāina.

5. E ʻauʻau ana ʻoukou i kēia lā?

6. Ke inu nei ke kinai ahi?
7. Ua pāʻani kou* papa i ke kakahiaka.

8. ʻŌlelo ke kupunakāne i ke kīwī.

__That man sells land.
__My dog is sitting in my car.
__Is the firefighter drinking?
__Your class played in the morning.
__They will ask the police officer.
__Will you all swim today?
__The grandfather speaks on the TV.
__Kanalu went sightseeing this morning.

Homework 5-5

Finish the following sentences by adding Centers. Color the Heads yellow and the Centers orange. Read your finished sentence out loud and translate.

   I. **Ke** 'ai **nei** . . .
   2. **Ua** hōʻike . . .
   3. **E** hele mai **ana** . . .
   4. **Ke** noho **nei** . . .
   5. Hana . . .
   6. **Ua** ʻōlelo . . .
   7. **Ke** pane **nei** . . .
   8. **Ua** pāʻani . . .
   9. **E** alakaʻi **ana** . . .
  10. Lawe mai . . .

Homework 5-6

Translate the following sentences. Color the **Heads** yellow and the **Centers** orange. Remember, some **Heads** will contain <u>no</u> verb tense markers.

  I. My friend sits.
  2. This boy is eating.
  3. She will read.
  4. The farmer ate.
  5. Nālei is answering.

  6. The doctor will stand.
  7. Her cat ran.
  8. That granddaughter played.
  9. They all are sightseeing.
10. Momi spoke.

Homework 5-7

Pick any yellow **verb** flashcard and an orange **noun** flashcard. Make a sentence without any verb markers. Rewrite the sentence with a past tense marker in the Head. Rewrite the sentence with present tense markers, then with future tense markers. Translate all four sentences.

c. The Third Sentence Section: Adding the Tail
Up to now, we have dealt with sentences that have only **Head** (verb) and **Center** (subject) sections. You should be very familiar with these

two sections at this point. Now we will add the third section to our Hawaiian sentence, the **Tail** or **object** section. Look at the English sentences in Homework 5-6 and add more information to each. What kind of information did you add?

They are sightseeing <u>on the Big Island</u>. This boy is eating <u>their goldfish</u>. She will read <u>the newspaper</u>. My friend sits <u>at the post office</u>.

The **Tail** section of a Hawaiian sentence adds prepositional phrases or objects that complete the meaning. Every Hawaiian sentence <u>must</u> have a **Head** and a **Center** section; the **Tail** section is required in only some sentences. Since not all sentences require a **Tail** section, it has a special attachment device. The sentence **Tail** section begins with **i**. You are familiar with name announcers and noun announcers; you may think of **i** as the **Tail announcer** if you wish. **I** means **in, on, to, at;** it appears at the beginning of every **Tail** section in our book. There are other kinds of **Tail announcers,** which you will learn later. Like <u>name</u> and <u>noun</u> announcers, our **Tail announcer** is an essential part of the sentence, even when we don't translate it into English.

How do we create a **Tail** section? For now, we will limit ourselves to using only the **Tail announcer** followed by a **noun annoucer plus noun** combination.

Head: **verb**	Center	Tail: **tail** announcer **+ noun** announcer **+ noun**
Hana	'o Waiola	**i kēlā haukapila.**
Inu	lākou	**i ka hōkele.**
Nānā	ke kumu	**i kona* haumāna.**

Homework 5-8

Complete the **Tail** section in these Hawaiian sentences. Follow the English translation and remember to **announce** your Tail!

1. You work <u>at the hospital</u>.   Hana 'oe_____.
2. Kanani sits <u>at the shopping center</u>.   Noho 'o Kanani_____.
3. The man looks <u>at his hand</u>.   Nānā ke kāne_____.
4. She eats <u>the poi</u>.   'Ai 'o ia_____.
5. That girl prays <u>in the morning</u>.   Pule kēlā kaikamahine____.
6. Keola runs <u>to the hotel</u>.   Holo 'o Keola_____.

7. His cousin sings <u>that song</u>.	Hīmeni kona hoahānau____.
8. I drink <u>this water</u>.	Inu wau____.
9. Winona lives <u>on this island</u>.	Nohoʻo Winona____.
10. My boy plays <u>at the party</u>.	Pāʻani koʻu* keikikāne.

Homework 5-9

Draw a circle around the **Center** in the Hawaiian sentences above. Underline the **Head**. Draw a line through the **Tail.** Now color the Center orange, the Head yellow, the Tail brown.

Homework 5-10

Translate the following into Hawaiian. Remember that the **Tail announcer** is <u>always</u> needed, even though it may not be indicated by the English sentence.

1. This lady works at the store.
2. Kōnane sees the mountain.
3. The captain sings on the ship.
4. She drinks in the afternoon.
5. Do you take a bath on Saturday?

III. ORAL REVIEW AND PRACTICE - DRILLS, DIALOGS, STORIES

a. Substitution Drills

Hana koʻu makuahine **i kēia halekūʻai.**		**Nānā** kākou	**i ke kīwī.**
ʻAi	ka hale ʻaina.	Heluhelu	i ka puke.
Noho	Waimea, Kauaʻi.	Lawaiʻa	i ke kai.
ʻŌlelo	ka ʻōlelo Hawaiʻi.	Kūʻai	i kona ʻāina.
Inu	ka wai hua ʻai.	Lawe mai	i ka iʻa.
Mahiʻai	Kaʻū, Hawaiʻi.	Hui	i Hāna, Maui.

<u>E noho ana</u>	ʻo ia i kēlā hōkele kahiko	i <u>Honokaʻa.</u>
Pāʻani	kona lumimoe	ka hale.
Ke manaʻo nei	ka hana	kēia ʻauinalā.
Ua heluhelu	ka nūpepa	ke kakahiaka.
Inu	ke kope	ke ahiahi.
E ʻai ana	ka ʻiʻo pipi ʻono	kēia lā.

b. Picture Practice

1. Look at the picture below. Make up a story to go along with the picture. What are the names of the people? How are they related? What do they say to each other?

 2. We've made up a story about Lehua and his father at the fishmarket.

Aia 'o Lehua a me kona makuakāne i ka mākeke i'a kaulana 'o Suisan i Hilo. Ke kū'ai nei nā lawai'a i nā 'ano i'a like 'ole o ke kai: 'o ke aku, 'o ke 'ahi, 'o ka 'ōpelu a pēlā aku.

Pāpā: E Lehua, e nānā i nā i'a!
Lehua: Hō ka nui o nā i'a! He aha ke 'ano o kēlā i'a 'ula'ula, e Pāpā?
Pāpā: He 'āweoweo kēlā, a he i'a 'ono loa!
Lehua: Ke kū'ai nei ka lawai'a i ka 'āweoweo i kēia mākeke i'a?
Pāpā: 'Ae. Ke kākau nei 'o ia i ke kumukū'ai i ka pepa. Ua 'ike 'oe?
Lehua: 'Ae. E 'ai ana kākou i kēlā i'a 'ono i kēia ahiahi, 'a'ole anei?

Lehua and his father are at the well-known fishmarket, Suisan, in Hilo. The fishermen are selling various kinds of fish of the sea: aku, 'ahi, 'ōpelu and so on.

Daddy: Lehua, look at the fish!
Lehua: Wow, so many fish. What kind of fish is that red fish, Daddy?
Daddy: That's an 'āweoweo, and it's a really delicious fish!
Lehua: Is the fisherman selling the 'āweoweo at this fishmarket?
Daddy: Yes. He's writing the price on the paper. Did you see?
Lehua: Yes. We're going to eat that delicious fish tonight, right?

c. **Listen and Learn**

Our new islands are Lānaʻi and Kahoʻolawe.

ʻO <u>Lānaʻi</u> kēia mokupuni. ʻO <u>Lānaʻi City</u> ke kūlanakauhale. He <u>'alani</u> ka waihoʻoluʻu no <u>Lānaʻi</u>. He lei <u>kaunaʻoa kahakai</u> kona lei. ʻO <u>Kaululūʻau</u> ke aliʻi kaulana no <u>Lānaʻi.</u> ʻO <u>Lānaʻihale</u> ke kuahiwi nani.

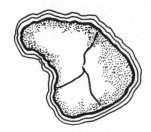

This island is <u>Lānaʻi</u>. <u>Lānaʻi City</u> is the town. The color of <u>Lānaʻi</u> is <u>orange.</u> Its lei is the <u>beach kaunaʻoa</u> lei. The famous chief of <u>Lānaʻi</u> is <u>Kaululūʻau.</u> The beautiful mountain is <u>Lānaʻihale.</u>

ʻO <u>Kahoʻolawe</u> kēia mokupuni. ʻAʻohe kūlanakauhale o <u>Kahoʻolawe.</u> He <u>'āhinahina</u> ka waihoʻoluʻu no <u>Kahoʻolawe.</u> He lei <u>hinahina kū kahakai</u> kona lei. ʻAʻohe aliʻi kaulana no <u>Kahoʻolawe.</u> ʻO <u>Luamakika</u> ke kuahiwi nani.

This island is <u>Kahoʻolawe</u>. Kahoʻolawe doesn't have a town. The color of <u>Kahoʻolawe</u> is <u>grey</u>. Its lei is the <u>beach hinahina</u> lei. There is no famous chief of <u>Kahoʻolawe</u>. The beautiful mountain is <u>Luamakika</u>.

Can you remember the names, color and lei for Moloka'i? Fill in the blanks; then read your story out loud. If you've forgotten any answers, instead of looking back to Chapter Four, find the Moloka'i story on the CD. Try to write down the Hawaiian words from <u>listening</u> only.

'O <u>Moloka'i</u> kēia mokupuni. 'O_____ke kūlanakauhale. He ka waiho'olu'u no_____. He lei _____kona lei. 'O___ke ali'i kaulana no_____. 'O_____ke kuahiwi nani.

As a further listening challenge, we offer a more difficult story about Lāna'i and Kaho'olawe. Listen along with the CD.

Lāna'i

Aia ma kekahi 'ao'ao o Lāna'i he mokupuni pali li'ili'i. Ua kapa 'ia kēia mokupuni pōhaku 'o Pu'upehe. He mo'olelo kaumaha loa kona. Ua aloha kekahi ali'i koa no Maui i kekahi wahine no Lāna'i. 'O Makakēhau ka inoa o ke ali'i koa. 'O Pu'upehe ka inoa o ka wahine. Ua noho 'o Makakēhau a me Pu'upehe ma kekahi ana kahakai ma Lāna'i. Ma kekahi lā, ua hele mai ka pō'ino; ua hao mai ka makani a ua nui nō nā nalu kai. Ua po'i mai kekahi nalu nui a ua komo i loko o ke ana kahakai. Ua piho-lo 'o Pu'upehe a make loa. Ua hāpai 'o Makakēhau i kona kino i ka mokupuni pali ki'eki'e. Ma laila 'o ia i kanu ai i ke kino o kāna wahine aloha. Ma hope, ua lele 'o Makakēhau i ke kai a ua make. Ke kipa aku 'oe i Lāna'i, e hele e nānā i ko Pu'upehe hē. Hiki ke 'ike 'ia ka hē ma luna o ka pali 'o Pu'upehe i kēia mau lā.

On one side of Lāna'i is a small island with steep cliffs. This rocky island is called Pu'upehe. It has a very sad story. A warrior chief from Maui loved a woman from Lāna'i. Makakēhau was the name of the warrior chief. Pu'upehe was the name of the woman. Makakēhau and Pu'upehe lived in a beach cave on Lāna'i. One day, a storm came up; the wind roared and the ocean waves were very large. A large wave broke and entered the cave. Pu'upehe drowned. Makakēhau carried her body up the steep cliffs of the island. There he buried the body of his beloved. Afterwards, Makakēhau jumped into the ocean and died. Whenever you visit Lāna'i, go and look at Pu'upehe's grave. A grave can be seen on top of the cliffs of Pu'upehe today.

Kaho'olawe

'O Kohemālamalamaokanaloa ka inoa kahiko o Kaho'olawe. He akua 'o Kanaloa no ka po'e kahiko. Aia ma Kaho'olawe ka lae 'o Kealaikahiki. Ua ha'alele nā wa'a o ka po'e kahiko iā Hawai'i nei i ka hahai 'ana i kēia lae.

The ancient name for Kaho'olawe is Kohemēlamalamaokanaloa. Kanaloa is a god of the ancient people. The point called Kealaikahiki (the way to Kahiki) is on Kaho'olawe. The canoes of the ancient people left Hawai'i by following this point.

d. Mele

This song mentions several important places on Lāna'i, such as Maunalei, Polihua, Lāna'ihale, and Kaunolū. It speaks of the island as a peaceful place, "like a bird soaring on the crest of the waves."

Lāna'i, He Manu Kīkaha
Music by Maxine Pua'ala Nu'uhiwa
Words by Randie Kamuela Fong

Ua la'i wale 'oe e Lāna'i
Me he manu kīkaha
I ke 'ale mālie

Ka noe hāli'i o Maunalei
He lei wehi 'oe
No Wahinekapu

Lu'u a ea 'o Polihua
Me nā honu 'ā'ī no'u
Pae a'e i ke one.

Niolo ke kuahiwi 'o Lāna'ihale
'O Kaululā'au,
Ka moho kaulana.

Kauha'a ke kai a'o Kaunolū
Ka nohona no ka Lani
I ka wā kūpuna.

Ha'ina ka puana no Lāna'i
Me he manu kīkaha
I ke 'ale mālie.

This song was written in support of young Hawaiians who opposed the military's use of Kahoʻolawe for bombing target practice and who went to the uninhabited island to reclaim it. The last line of the song urges Hawaiians to move forward until there is victory for Kahoʻolawe. After many years of protest, the bombing of Kahoʻolawe has recently stopped.

Mele o Kahoʻolawe, by Harry Mitchell

Aloha kuʻu moku ʻo Kahoʻolawe
Mai kinohi kou inoa ʻo Kanaloa
Kohemālamalama lau kanaka ʻole
Hiki mai nā pua e hoʻomalu mai

Alu like kākou lāhui Hawaiʻi
Mai ka lā hiki mai i ka lā kau aʻe
Kū paʻa a hahai hōikaika nā kānaka
Kau liʻi mākou, nui ke aloha no ka ʻāina

Hanohano nā pua o Hawaiʻi nei
No ke kaua kauholo me ke aupuni
Paʻa pū ka manaʻo no ka pono o ka ʻāina
I mua nā oua lanakila Kahoʻolawe.

Chapter Six

AIA SENTENCE PATTERNS: WHERE ARE YOU?

I. ORAL WORK SECTION

a. Hakalama Here is a variation of the Hakalama with two vowels presented in the last chapter. Be sure to pronounce the first vowel clearly before you blend it into the second.

Hai	Kai	Lai	Mai	Nai	Pai	Wai
Hei	Kei	Lei	Mei	Nei	Pei	Wei
Hoi	Koi	Loi	Moi	Noi	Poi	Woi
Hui	Kui	Lui	Mui	Nui	Pui	Wui
Hie	Kie	Lie	Mie	Nie	Pie	Wie
Hiu	Kiu	Liu	Miu	Niu	Piu	Wiu

b. Vocabulary

Nouns

ke **kahuna**	expert, priest
ka **mana**	spiritual power
ke **kahunapule**	minister
ka **halepule**	church
ka **pule**	prayer, week
ka **mahina**	moon, month
ka **makahiki**	year
ke **ola**	life
ka **make**	death
ka **pilikia**	problem
ka **pō**	night, darkness
ke **ao**	daytime, cloud
ka **holoholona**	animal
ka **pōpoki**	cat
ka **'īlio**	dog
ka **wa'a**	canoe
ka **hoe**	paddle
ka **papa he'enalu**	surfboard

Verbs

pule	to pray
kōkua	to help
'au'au	to bathe, swim
holo	to run
mana'o	to think
hānau	to give birth
hoe	to paddle
he'enalu	to surf
mālama	to take care of
ho'oponopono	to fix, repair
lele	to jump
ho'i	to return, go back
ho'i mai	to come back
komo	to enter
wehe	to open
pani	to close
honi	to kiss, smell
ho'olohe	to listen

c. Useful Phrases

1. kēia mau pōpoki	these cats
2. nā pōpoki	the cats
3. kēlā mau holoholona	those animals
4. nā holoholona	the animals
5. i kēia lā	today
6. i ka lā ‘apōpō	tomorrow
7. i kēia pule	this week
8. i nehinei	yesterday
9. i kēia kakahiaka	this morning
10. i kēia ahiahi	this evening

Aia kou* mau ‘īlio i ka hale?
Are your dogs at home?
Aia kēia mau makuakāne i ka hana.
These fathers are at work.
Aia ka papa hou i kēia pule.
The new class is this week.
Kōkua ke kahunapule i nā keiki ‘ilihune.
The minister helps the poor children.
Mālama nā mo‘opuna i ka ‘ōlelo Hawai‘i.
The grandchildren (descendants) take care of the Hawaiian language.

d. Dialogs

1. <u>Kamaʻilio ʻo Leialoha me Mahina</u>.
Mahina: Aia i hea kou* mau pōpoki i kēia ahiahi?
Leialoha: ʻAʻole maopopo iaʻu. Aia lākou ma ka pā hale?
Mahina: ʻAʻole. Manaʻo au, aia nā pōpoki i ke kahakai. E nānā!
Leialoha: Holo nā pōpoki i ke one. Lele nō hoʻi lākou!
Mahina: Auē nō hoʻi! Ke ʻai nei kou* mau pōpoki ʻeleu i ka manu!

<u>Leialoha talks with Mahina</u>.
Mahina: Where are your cats this evening?
Leialoha: I don't know. Are they in the yard?
Mahina: No. I think the cats are on the beach. Look!
Leialoha: The cats run in the sand. They also jump.
Mahina: Goodness sakes! Your lively cats are eating the bird!

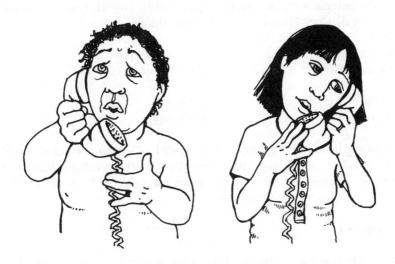

2. <u>Kamaʻilio ʻo Mamo me Mikiʻoi</u>.
Mamo: Aia i hea ke kahunapule?
Mikiʻoi: Aʻo ʻo ia i ka papa heluhelu Paipala i ka pōʻahā. He aha ka
    pilikia?
Mamo: Aia koʻu* mau keikikāne i ka halemākaʻi. Ua ʻaihue lākou i ka
    papa heʻenalu i nehinei.
Mikiʻoi: Nui ka pilikia! E kelepona ana au i ka halepule. Hoʻolohe nā
    keikikāne kolohe i ke kahunapule.
Mamo: Mahalo nō! He kōkua nui kēlā.

<u>Mamo talks with Miki'oi.</u>
Mamo: Where's the minister?
Miki'oi: He teaches a Bible reading class on Thursday. What's the
    problem?
Mamo: My boys are at the police station. They stole a surfboard
    yesterday.
Miki'oi: Lots of trouble! I'll phone the church. Rascal boys listen to the
    minister.
Mamo: Many thanks! That's a big help!

II. GRAMMAR SECTION

a. Pluralizing Noun Announcers
So far, all noun announcers have been singular. Now we can expand
our language by pluralizing common nouns. Look at the Hawaiian and
English sentences below. What do you add to English nouns to make
them plural? Does Hawaiian do the same thing?

ke kumuniu	the coconut tree
nā kumuniu	the coconut tree**s**
ka i'a	the fish
nā i'a	the fish**es**

We can see from these examples that while English **nouns** change their
form to make a plural, Hawaiian nouns do not. To pluralize a Hawaiian
noun, we change the form of the **noun announcer.** Both **ke** and **ka**
change to **nā** as their plural form.

Self-Test 6-1

Choose any five nouns from your orange noun flashcards. Say
the correct singular form of the noun announcer **the** that goes
with each Hawaiian noun; then pluralize that noun. What is the
English translation? Only **ke** and **ka** change to **nā** to form the plural. All
other **noun announcers** simply squeeze in the word **mau** between the
noun announcer and **noun.** Look at the following examples.

kona hale 'aina	his restautant
kona **mau** hale 'aina	his restaurants
kou wāwae	your foot
kou **mau** wāwae	your **feet**

| ko'u inoa | my name |
| ko'u **mau** inoa | my name<u>s</u> |

Notice that while the noun announcers **kēia** and **kēlā** simply add **mau** to form a plural noun, their plural forms are translated differently than their singular forms.**

kēia 'āina	this land
<u>kēia</u> **mau** 'āina	**these** land<u>s</u>
kēlā heiau	that temple
<u>kēlā</u> **mau** heiau	**those** temple<u>s</u>

Self-Test 6-2

Choose any five orange noun flashcards. Use only **kēia** and **kēlā** to announce each noun. Now add **mau**. Translate both singular and plural noun announcer plus noun combinations into English. Work with a partner: choose five more noun flashcards and have your partner pluralize them with **mau**. Next, say some English singular and plural nouns with **these, those, this, that.** Have your partner say them in Hawaiian.

Homework 6-1

Add nouns to the following **plural noun announcers.** Translate into English.

I. nā_____   3. kēia mau_____   5. kēlā mau_____
2. kona mau_____   4. ko'u mau_____   6. kou mau_____

** Although **kēia** or **kēlā** may stand alone in the Center, **kēia mau** or **kēlā mau** must always be followed by a noun.

Homework 6-2

Matching. Write the number of the Hawaiian phrase next to its English translation.

1. kēia mau pālule aloha	___ the lanterns
2. nā pākaukau	___ his parents
3. ko'u mau hoahānau	___ these aloha shirts
4. kēlā mau pahi	___ your guava trees
5. nā kukuihelepō	___ the post offices
6. kona mau mākua	___ those little fishes
7. kēia mau pūpū	___ those knives
8. kou* mau kumukuawa	___ the tables
9. nā haleleka	___ my cousins
10. kēlā mau i'a li'ili'i	___ these shells

Homework 6-3

Pluralize the following phrases. Translate the pluralized phrase into English.

1. kēia makahiki	6. kēia pō
2. ka holoholona	7. kona* kālā
3. kou* hoe	8. ka 'īlio
4. kēlā papa he'enalu	9. ko'u lā hānau
5. ke kahunapule	10. ke kama'āina

b. Aia Locational Pattern

Our new **Aia locational** sentence pattern tells where someone or something is.

Aia ka pōpoki i ka haukapila.	The cat is in the hospital.
Aia wau i ka hana.	I'm at work.
Aia 'o Heanu i ka noho.	Heanu is in the chair.

Let's divide these sentences into three sections. There should be only <u>one</u> word in the **Head.** What is it?

<u>Head: Aia</u>	<u>Center</u>	<u>Tail: i + noun announcer + noun</u>
Aia	ka pōpoki	i ka haukapila
Aia	wau	i ka hana
Aia	'o Heanu	i ka noho

The Aia locational sentence is easy to put together, because the **Head** is always **Aia.** This word gives the idea of something being located someplace. It is not usually translated into English, although its meaning is present in the English sentence. Aia sentences can also be used to tell **when** something is. This new pattern is also the first we've learned that <u>always</u> requires a **Tail** section. That's because the **Tail of** an **Aia locational** sentence holds the key information: **when** or **where** something or someone is.

The cat is <u>in the hospital</u>.   I am <u>at work.</u>   Heanu is <u>on the chair</u>.

Homework 6-4

Finish the following **Aia locational** sentences by adding a Tail section. Don't forget to start with the **tail announcer.**

1. Aia 'oe_____.
2. Aia 'o Keoni_____.
3. Aia kela mahi'ai_____.
4. Aia lākou_____.
5. Aia ka papa_____.

Homework 6-5

Matching. Write the number of the Hawaiian sentence next to the correct translation.

1. Aia kēia keiki i ke kahua pā'ani.   __ No. The car is on the street.
2. Aia 'o ia i kona halekū'ai.   __ Where's my comb?
3. Aia 'o Momi i 'ane'i   __ Yes. He's at work.
4. Aia ka hālāwai i ka hola 'eono.   __ This child is on the playground.
5. Aia ke ka'a i ka haleka'a?   __ Is Palani at work?
6. 'A'ole. Aia ke ka'a i ke alanui.   __ She's at her store.
7. Aia i hea ko'u* kahi?   __ The meeting is at six o'clock.
8. Aia kou* kahi i ka pākaukau.   __ Momi's here.
9. Aia 'o Palani i ka hana?   __ Is the car in the garage?
10. 'Ae. Aia 'o ia i ka hana.   __ Your comb is on the table.

Homework 6-6

 Translate the following sentences into Hawaiian.

1. His son is at school.
2. Kanoni is in her bedroom.
3. That plumeria is in my lei.
4. Is that plumeria in my lei?
5. The test is at church.

6. You are in my house!
7. Is the class this evening?
8. No. The class is this noon time.
9. Hulali is at the post office.
10. This cat is on your leg.

c. Asking Questions with the Aia Locational Pattern
Look over the sentences above and think about how to ask questions with the **Aia locational** sentences. As with many Hawaiian sentence patterns, we can simply keep the same word order, but change our voice intonation to ask a question. However, with the **Aia locational** pattern, adding a question mark to the end of a statement indicates that we are <u>guessing</u> where someone or something is. Is the car <u>in the garage</u>? Is Palani <u>at work</u>? To ask directly **where** someone or something is, we use the question phrase **Aia i hea.**

Aia i hea ʻoe?	Where are you?
Aia i hea ka lūʻau?	Where's the lūʻau?
Aia i hea kēlā puke?	Where's that book?
Aia i hea ʻo Honouliuli?	Where's Honouliuli?

As in English, this question can be used to ask where places like Honouliuli are, as well as people or things.

Self-Test 6-3

Can you divide these questions into **Center** and **Head** sections? Color the Centers orange and the Heads green.

The **Center** contains the person, place, or thing we're talking about. Did you discover that the **Head** of this question pattern must contain the phrase **Aia i hea?** <u>Maikaʻi!</u>

Now make up answers to these questions. How many sections will your answers have? What goes in the **Head** section of your answer? **Aia** indicates location; <u>i hea</u> adds the question word **where.** Therefore, when we answer the question, we drop the **i hea (where)** and only **Aia** remains in the Head.

Head	Center	Tail
Aia **i hea**	'oe?	
Aia	wau	i ke kikowaenakū'ai.
Aia **i hea**	kēlā puke?	
Aia	kēlā puke?	i ka lumimoe.
Aia **i hea**	'o Pohukaina?	
Aia	'o Pohukaina?	i Kaka'ako.
Aia **i hea**	ka lū'au	
Aia	ka lū'au	i ka halepule.

Notice that **where** questions have only **Head** and **Center** sections, while their answers require a **Tail** section. The **Tail** contains the essential information, telling us where the Center subject is.

III. ORAL REVIEW AND PRACTICE - DRILLS, DIALOGS, STORIES

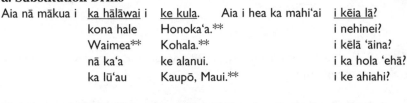

a. Substitution Drills

Aia nā mākua i	ka hālāwai i	ke kula.	Aia i hea ka mahi'ai	i kēia lā?
	kona hale	Honoka'a.**		i nehinei?
	Waimea**	Kohala.**		i kēlā 'āina?
	nā ka'a	ke alanui.		i ka hola 'ehā?
	ka lū'au	Kaupō, Maui.**		i ke ahiahi?

Ua hele wau i	Hau'ula** i	nehinei.	Holoi kākou i	nā puna i	ka lumikuke
	ke kauka	Ala Moana.**		nā 'īlio	ka pā hale.
	Kaua'i**	ka mokulele.		nā pua	ka ua.
	ka hana	kēia lā.		nā kāwele	'ane'i.
	Kailua**	ke ka'a hou.		nā pā	kēia awakea.

**place names

b. Picture Practice

1. Look at the picture below. Make up a story to go along with the picture. What are the names of the people? How are they related? What do they say to each other?

 2. We've made up a story about Lahela and her parents planting puakenikeni trees.

Aia nā mākua o Lahela i ka māla pua ma uka o ka hale. Ke ʻeli nei ka makuakāne i ka lepo. E kanu ana ka makuahine i nā kumupuakenikeni.

Pāpā: E Lahela, e hāʻawi mai i ke kopalā, ke ʻoluʻolu.
Lahela: Aia i hea ke kopalā, e Pāpā?
Pāpā: Aia ke kopalā i koʻu kalaka. ʻIke ʻoe?
Lahela: ʻAe. Eiʻa, e Pāpā. He aha ke ʻano o kēia mau kumu, e Māmā?
Māmā: He mau kumupuakenikeni kēia, e ke kaikamahine. He pua ʻaʻala
    ka puakenikeni. E kanu ana au i kēia mau kumupuakenikeni i kēia lā.
Lahela: Maikaʻi! Nui koʻu makemake i ka puakenikeni.

Lahela's parents are in the flower garden upland of the house. The father is digging in the dirt. The mother is going to plant puakenikeni trees.

Daddy: Lahela, give me the shovel, please.
Lahela: Where's the shovel, Daddy?
Daddy: The shovel's in my truck. Do you see it?
Lahela: Yes. Here, Daddy. What kind of trees are these, Mommy?

Mommy: These are puakenikeni trees, daughter. The puakenikeni is a
   sweet-smelling flower. I will plant these puakenikeni trees today.
Lahela: Good! I really like puakenikeni.

c. Listen and Learn

Our new island is Maui.

'O <u>Maui</u> kēia mokupuni. 'O <u>Wailuku</u> ke kūlanakauhale. He <u>'ākala</u> ka waiho'olu'u no <u>Maui.</u> He lei <u>lokelani</u> kona lei. 'O <u>Pi'ilani</u> ke ali'i kaulana no
Maui. 'O Haleakalā ke kuahiwi nani.

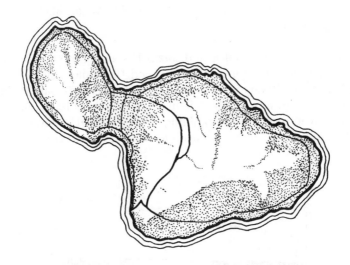

This island is <u>Maui</u>. <u>Wailuku</u> is the town. The color of <u>Maui</u> is <u>pink</u>. Its
lei is the <u>lokelani</u> lei. The famous chief of <u>Maui</u> is <u>Pi'ilani</u>. The beautiful
mountain is <u>Haleakalā</u>.

Can you remember the names, color and lei for Lānaʻi? for Kahoʻolawe?
Fill in the blanks; then read your story out loud. If you've forgotten any
answers, instead of looking back to Chapter Five, find the Lānaʻi and
Kahoʻolawe stories on the CD. Try to write down the Hawaiian words
from <u>listening</u> only.

'O <u>Lānaʻi</u> kēia mokupuni. 'O_____ke kūlanakauhale. He_____
ka waihoʻoluʻu no_____. He lei_____ kona lei. 'O_____ ke aliʻi
kaulana no_____. 'O_____ke kuahiwi nani.

'O Kaho'olawe kēia mokupuni. 'A'ohe kūlanakauhale o Kaho'olawe. He
_____ka waiho'olu'u no_____. He lei _____ kona lei. 'A'ohe ali'i
kaulana no_____. 'O_____ke kuahiwi nani.

As a further listening challenge, we offer a more complicated
story about Maui. Listen to the CD and read along.

He mokupuni nani loa 'o Maui. Nui nā kuahiwi a nui nō ho'i nā awāwa
o Maui. No laila, ua kapa 'ia 'o Maui ka mokupuni o nā awāwa. Aia ma
Hāna ka heiau nui loa o Hawai'i nei. He kanahā a 'oi kapua'i ke ki'eki'e
o nā paia o kēlā heiau, 'o Pi'ilanihale. 'O Pi'ilani ke ali'i kaulana o Maui.
Nāna i alaka'i i ke kūkulu 'ana i ka heiau. Nāna nō ho'i i kauoha i ke
kūkulu 'ana i ke alanui kahiko i hele a puni 'o Maui. Hiki ke 'ike 'ia kēlā
alanui kahiko i kēia la.

Maui is a very beautiful island. Maui has many mountains and also
many valleys. Therefore, Maui is called the Valley Isle. The biggest
heiau here in Hawai'i is in Hāna. The walls of that heiau, Pi'ilanihale,
are forty feet or more high. Pi'ilani is the famous chief of Maui. He was
the one who directed the building of the heiau. He also ordered the
building of the ancient road around Maui. This old road can be seen
today.

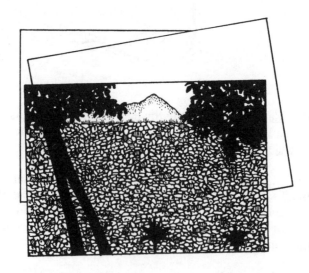

d. Mele

This lively song speaks of the beauty of Haleakalā, which dominates
east Maui. It mentions the "upcountry" town of Makawao on the slopes
of the mountain and the chilly 'ūkiu wind and rain of that area.

Haleakalā (composer unknown)

Kuahiwi nani 'oe Haleakalā
Kaulana ho'i 'oe kū kilakila

'O Makawao ia ua kaulana
E ka 'ohi e ka iho o ka lā'au

He 'ūkiu e ka ua o ka 'āina
Me ka makani aheahe 'olu'olu

Puana ka inoa a i lohe 'ia
Kuahiwi nani 'oe Haleakalā.

'O IDENTIFICATION PATTERN AND A BRIEF LOOK BACK

I. ORAL WORK SECTION

a. Hakalama Here is our last variation on the Hakalama chart. It is another variation on the combination of two vowels.

Heo	Keo	Leo	Meo	Neo	Peo	Weo
Hio	Kio	Lio	Mio	Nio	Pio	Wio
Huo	Kuo	Luo	Muo	Nuo	Puo	Wuo
Hoe	Koe	Loe	Moe	Noe	Poe	Woe
Hou	Kou	Lou	Mou	Nou	Pou	Wou

b. Vocabulary

Nouns		Verbs	
ke **kukui**	light, lamp	**helu**	to count
ka **uila**	electricity	**heluhelu**	to read
ke **kīwī**	television	**kākau**	to write
ka **lēkiō**	radio	**kali**	to wait
ka **noho**	chair	**mahiʻai**	to farm
ka **pākaukau**	table	**lawaiʻa**	to fish
ka **ʻaina**	meal	**nānā**	to watch, look
ka **hale ʻaina**	restaurant	**hāpai**	to lift up, carry
ke **kuene**	waiter/waitress	**uē**	to cry
ka **mea ʻai**	food	**lawe mai**	to bring
ka **mea inu**	drink	**lawe aku**	to take
ka **wai**	water	**ʻaihue**	to steal
ka **ʻōpala**	garbage	**hānai**	to raise, feed
ke **kaʻa**	car	**ʻakaʻaka**	to laugh
ke **alanui**	street	**holoi**	to wash
ka **mokulele**	plane	**kamaʻilio**	to converse
ke **kikiki**	ticket	**hiamoe**	to sleep
ke **kahua mokulele**	airport	**ala**	to wake up

c. Useful Phrases

'ekahi	one	ka pō'akahi	Monday
'elua	two	ka pō'alua	Tuesday
'ekolu	three	ka pō'akolu	Wednesday
'ehā	four	ka pō'ahā	Thursday
'elima	five	ka pō'alima	Friday
'eono	six	ka pō'aono	Saturday
'ehiku	seven	ka lāpule	Sunday
'ewalu	eight	i ka pō'ahā	on Thursday
'eiwa	nine	i ka pō'akahi	on Monday
'umi	ten	i ka lāpule	on Sunday

ka 'aina kakahiaka	breakfast
ka 'aina awakea	lunch
ka 'aina ahiahi	dinner

E hiamoe ana ka pēpē i ka mokulele.
The baby will sleep on the airplane.

Ua lawe aku ke kuene i ka 'ōpala.
The waitress took away the garbage.

Holo nā ka'a ma ke alanui. Holo na wa'a ma ke kai.
The cars run on the street. The canoes travel on the sea.

d. Dialogs

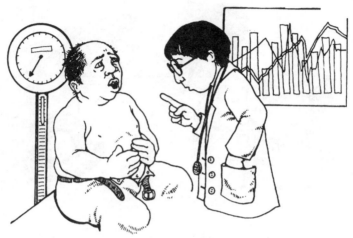

1. <u>Kamaʻilio ke kauka me ke kanaka maʻi.</u>
Ke kanaka maʻi: ʻO Kauka Kamanō ʻoe?
Ke kauka: ʻAe. ʻO au ke kauka. Maʻi ʻoe?
Ke kanaka maʻi: Maʻi nō au, e ke kauka. ʻEha koʻu ʻōpū.
Ke kauka: Ua ʻai nui ʻoe i ka pō nei?
Ke kanaka maʻi: ʻAe. Ua hele au i ka lūʻau i nehinei. Ua ʻono ka puaʻa
    kālua.
Ke kauka: ʻO kēia ka lūʻau maikaʻi. Mai ʻai hou i kēia lā!
Ke kanaka maʻi: ʻAe. Mahalo, e ke kauka.

<u>The doctor talks with the sick person.</u>
The sick person: Are you Dr. Kamanō?
The doctor: Yes, I'm the doctor. Are you sick?
The sick person: I'm really sick, doctor. My stomach is sore.
The doctor: Did you eat a lot last night?
The sick person: Yes. I went to a lūʻau yesterday. The kālua pig was
    delicious!
The doctor: This is good medicine. Don't eat again
    today! The sick person: Yes. Thank you, doctor.

2. <u>Kamaʻilio ke kinai ahi me ke kāne.</u>
Ke kinai ahi: ʻO kou kaʻa kēia kaʻa hou?
Ke kāne: ʻAe. ʻO koʻu* makana lā hānau kēia kaʻa ʻulaʻula.
Ke kinai ahi: ʻO kēia kou lā hanau?
Ke kāne: ʻAe. ʻO kēia koʻu lā hānau. E mālama ana koʻu ʻohana i ka
    pāʻina i kēia ahiahi.
Ke kinai ahi: Auē! Hauʻoli Lā Hānau! Mai inu nui ʻoe. Mai hanaʻino i
    kou kaʻa hou.
Ke kāne: He manaʻo kūpono kēlā. E mālama pono ana au i koʻu kaʻa
    hou.

<u>The firefighter talks with the man.</u>
The firefighter: Is this new car your car?
The man: Yes. This red car is my birthday present.
The firefighter: Is this your birthday?
The man: Yes. This is my birthday. My family is throwing a party this
    evening.
The firefighter: Wow! Happy Birthday! Don't drink a lot. Don't abuse
    your new car.
The man: That's an appropriate thought. I'll take good care of my new
    car.

II. GRAMMAR SECTION
This is our last chapter and we will use it partially to review what
you've learned. However, let's learn our last major sentence pattern
first.

a. ʻO Identification Sentence: A Step Beyond ʻO wai kou inoa?

Look back over the statements we can make with the **He plus noun** pattern. How do you say "This is **a** friendʻ? Do you remember the translation tricks that help us divide up the English sentence into **Center** and **Head?** What do you do first with the English sentence? What's next? Review all the steps in translating: cross out **is/are,** find the Center, use **a** as a clue that our Hawaiian sentence will start with **He.** What's the result? **He hoaaloha kēia** is the correct translation. The **He plus noun** pattern is a very useful tool, but is limited to translating sentences that have **a/an** plus noun in English.

What if you want to say "This is **my** friend" or "This is **that** friend"? You would use the same translation tricks discussed in Chapter Four. First place the words that come before **is** into the **Center** section; then cross out **is.**

| | **Center** |
| | This |

Place what's left in the English sentence into the **Head.**

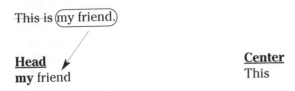

| **Head** | **Center** |
| **my** friend | This |

Now translate into Hawaiian.

This is my friend.

Head	**Center**
my friend	This
koʻu hoaaloha	kēia.

The Hawaiian sentence is not yet finished. We must add **ʻO** to the beginning of the sentence to signal that this is an **ʻO identification** sentence. Our complete sentence should be **ʻO koʻu hoaaloha kēia.** Like its cousin the **name announcer,** the **ʻO identification announcer** is never translated into English, but is essential to the meaning of the Hawaiian sentence. It announces that this is an **ʻO identification** sentence.

Self Test 7-1

Pick any orange **noun** flashcard. Use it and any **noun announc-er** you choose to complete the **Head** in the following sentences. Don't forget to **announce** your sentences!

Head: ʻO + noun announcer + noun	Center
_____	kēlā kāne
_____	kona* mea ʻai.
_____	ʻoia.
_____	ʻo Keʻala.

Look at how the **ʻo** is used in this sentence: " **ʻO koʻu makuahine ʻo Keʻala. Keʻala is my mother.**" In the Center, the **name announcer** focuses attention on the subject's name. In the Head, the **ʻO identifica-tion announcer** shows that an identifying **noun** about Keʻala is coming up: She is **koʻu makuahine**.

Homework 7-1

Matching. Write the number of the Hawaiian sentence next to its English translation.

1. ʻO Maile kou makuahine.
2. ʻO kēia hale ʻaina ʻo ka Willows.
3. ʻO kēlā mea heʻenalu ka mea akamai.
4. ʻO ka wai ʻalani ka mea inu?
5. ʻO kēia ʻuala kona* ʻaina awakea.
6. ʻO ka noho ʻoluʻolu kēia.
7. ʻO Beretania ke alanui kaulana.
8. ʻO kona* lēkiō kēlā lēkiō.
9. ʻO Puʻuloa ʻo Pearl Harbor.
10. ʻO ka mahiʻai kona* hana.

__ That radio is his radio.
__ Pearl Harbor is Puʻuloa.*
__ This is the comfortable chair.
__ His work is farming.
__ The Willows is this restaurant.
__ The smart one is that surfer.
__ Your mother is Maile.
__ Her lunch is this sweet potato.
__ Is the drink orange juice?
__ The famous street is Beretania.

* Puʻuloa is the Hawaiian name for Pearl Harbor.

Homework 7-2

a. Translate the following sentence with the **ʻO identification** pattern.

1. That woman is the teacher.
2. This is your job.
3. I am the newcomer.
4. Nāʻala is that strong captain.

5. Is Nāʻala that strong captain?
6. The poi is his food.
7. That is the pretty lei.
8. She is my mother.
9. You are her grandfather.
10. Nāihe is the aliʻi today.

b. Commands

E hele mai!	Come here!	**Mai** hele mai!	Don't come here!
E hele!	Go!	**Mai** hele!	Don't go!
E komo mai!	Enter! Come in!	**Mai** komo mai!	Don't come in!
E heluhelu!	Read!	**Mai** heluhelu!	Don't read!

Commanding others to do or not to do something is simple. Pick any yellow **verb** flashcard. Add the **do command** word **E** before the **verb**. If you <u>don't want</u> someone to do something, use the **don't command** word **Mai** before the verb.

Self-Test 7-2

Pick any five yellow verb flashcards and command someone to do, then not to do that action. As in English commands, the subject of Hawaiian commands is understood to be the pronoun **you**. Simple commands are just **Heads**.

Head: do/don't plus verb

E inu!	Drink!
Mai nānā!	Don't look!
E ʻōlelo!	Speak!
Mai ʻaihue!	Don't steal!

Homework 7-3

 Matching. Write the number of the Hawaiian command next to its translation.

1. E hāpai i ka 'ōpala!
2. Mai nānā aku i ke kīwī!
3. E hānai i nā 'īlio i kēia 'auinalā!
4. Mai 'aihue i kona ka'a!
5. Mai 'aka'aka aku i kou hoahānau!
6. E kama'ilio i ke kumu.
7. Mai uē, e ka pēpē!

___ Don't laugh at your cousin!
___ Feed the dogs this afternoon!
___ Carry the garbage!
___ Don't watch TV!
___ Don't cry, baby!
___ Talk to the teacher!
___ Don't steal her car!

c. Adding Tails to Our Sentence Patterns

Look back once more at the kinds of **Tails** you've learned about. In which sentence patterns are they required? (in some **Action** sentences, in <u>all</u> **Aia** sentences). Most of the time, however, **Tails** are optional. If they're optional, can they be added to any of our five sentence patterns? Yes! **Tails** add more information and make our simple sentences more sophisticated. Can you think of an English sentence that has more than one **Tail?** Of course! We go *to church* <u>in Ka'a'awa</u>. <u>In Ka'a'awa</u> is a **Tail** and so is *to church*. While a simple Hawaiian sentence will contain only one **Head** and only one **Center** section, we can add **any** number of **Tail** sections. That's how to add more information to our simple sentence patterns.

Homework 7-4

Make up five **Action** sentences and add any of these **Tails** to each sentence.

1. i kēia 'auinalā
2. i ka mokulele
3. i ke ali'i
4. i ke kinai ahi
5. i ka pō'alima
6. i ke kakahiaka
7. i ka hale 'aina
8. i ko'u* kumu
9. i ke kālā

Homework 7-5

Below are several incomplete sentences. Make up at least two **Tail** sections to add to each. Translate the completed sentence into English. Remember to announce each Tail!

1. Aia ko'u kupunawahine . . .
2. Ua hele kākou . . .

3. Māluhiluhi ke kauka . . .
4. He aha kēlā . . . ?
5. O wai ka inoa o kēia kāpena . . . ?
6. Aia 'o Kalani . . .
7. Ke pā'ani nei nā keikikāne . . .
8. Aia ka hālāwai . . .
9. Aia i hea kēlā mau pua . . . ?
10. Akamai nā haumāna . . .

d. Reviewing Head, Center, Tail
You are now familiar with the three sections that our simple sentences can be divided into. Use the following questions as a review of what you've learned about the parts and function of each section. If there are any questions you can't answer, look back over the **Grammar Section** of Chapters One through Six until you find the answer.

1. Name the three sections of a Hawaiian sentence.
2. What two sections are common to **all** Hawaiian sentences?
3. Which section comes first in a Hawaiian sentence?
4. When and why do we need the third section?

Center
1. What are the three kinds of subjects in the **Center** section?
2. What is a **noun announcer?** Where is it used? Why is it necessary?
3. What is a **name announcer?** Where is it used? Why is it necessary?
4. Name all singular Hawaiian pronouns. Translate into English.
5. Name all plural Hawaiian pronouns we've learned. Translate.
6. Why do we start from the **Center** when translating from Hawaiian to English or vice versa?

Head
1. How is the **Head** section related to word order in an English sentence?
2. What is the function of the **Head** section and why is it important?
3. Name five different kinds of **Heads** and the sentence pattern each begins.

Tail
1. What is the function of the **Tail** section and why is it important?
2. What is a **Tail announcer?** How is it used?
3. How is a **Tail** section formed?

e. Five simple sentence patterns
Use the following questions as a guide to your own review of the sentence patterns you've learned.

The **descriptive** sentence
1. What kind of word goes in the **descriptive** sentence **Head**?
2. What type of information does this sentence pattern give us?
3. Using your green flashcards, make up three **descriptive** sentences.

The **He aha** sentence
1. How does the **He plus noun** pattern relate to its English translation?
2. What is the English clue that tells us to use the **He aha** pattern?
3. Using your orange flashcards, make up three **he aha kēia** questions; then answer your questions.

The **Action** sentence pattern
1. What goes in the **Head** of an action sentence?
2. What are the Hawaiian tense markers and what section are they in?
3. How many sections are possible in an **Action** sentence?

The **Aia** sentence pattern
1. What kind of information does the **Aia** sentence pattern give us?
2. What goes in the **Head** of an **Aia** sentence?
3. Why is a **Tail** needed in every **Aia** sentence?
4. What are the two ways to ask questions with **Aia** sentences?

The **'O identification** pattern
1. What kind of information does the 'O identification sentence tell us?
2. How does the **'o** function in the Head and Center of this sentence pattern?
3. Both **'O identification** and **He aha** patterns are used to identify something or someone. How are the two patterns different?

III. ORAL REVIEW AND PRACTICE - DRILLS, DIALOGS, STORIES

a. Substitution Drills

'O keia lei puakenikeni	kona lei.	'O ko'u hoaaloha	'o ia.
kēia	ka laiki.	ke kāne	'o Moke
ka mahimahi	kēlā i'a.	ke kahunapule	ko'u*keikikāne.
ke kupuna	'o 'Ululani.	kēlā	ka wahine nani.
kona wa'a	kēia wa'a.	kou halekula	kēia?
ko'u* mo'opuna	kēia.	ke ali'i	'oe.

Mai	hānai	'oe	i	ka pōpoki!	E	holo	'oukou!
	hāpai			ka pēpē!		hīmeni	
	'ōlelo			ka 'ōlelo Haole!		hula	
	kākau			ka paia.		nānā mai	
	lele			ka moe!		pule	
	'au			kēia kahakai!		pā'ani	

b. Picture Practice

1. Look at the picture below. Make up a story to go along with the picture. What are the names of the people? How are they related? What do they say to each other?

 2. We've made up a story about a policeman who thinks he's caught a thief. Listen to the story on the CD several times.

Ua hopu ka mākaʻi i kekahi kāne i ka halekūʻai i ka pō nei. Manaʻo ka mākaʻi, ua ʻaihue ke kāne i ke kālā.

Ka mākaʻi: He aha kēia? ʻO kou* kēlā kēia?

Ke kāne: ʻAe. ʻO koʻu* kālā kēia. He kanaka waiwai au.

Ka mākaʻi: Auē! Mai hoʻopunipuni! Ua ʻike au iā ʻoe i loko o ka halekūʻai i ka pō nei. ʻO ke kālā kēia mai ka halekūʻai mai. Ua ʻaihuo ʻoe i kēia?

Ke kāne: ʻAʻole! ʻO kēlā halekūʻai koʻu halekūʻai. ʻO ʻOʻoka koʻu inoa. ʻO wai ka inoa o ka halekūʻai?

Ka mākaʻi: Auē! ʻO ʻOʻoka Superette ka inoa o ka halekūʻai. ʻO ʻOʻoka nō hoʻi kou inoa? E kala mai!

The policeman caught a man in a store last night. The policeman thinks the man has stolen money.

Policeman: What's this? Is this your money?

Man: Yes, that's my money. I'm a rich man.

Policeman: Gosh! Don't lie! I saw you inside the store last night. This is the money from the store. Did you steal this?

Man: No! That store is my store. My name is ʻOʻoka. What's the name of the store?

Policeman: Oops! The name of the store is ʻOʻoka Superette. ʻOʻoka is also your name? I'm sorry!

c. Listen and Learn

Our new island is Hawai'i.

'O <u>Hawai'i</u> kēia mokupuni. 'O <u>Hilo</u> ke kūlanakauhale. He <u>'ula'ula</u> ka waiho'olu'u no <u>Hawai'i</u>. He lei <u>lehua</u> kona lei. 'O <u>Keawe</u> ke ali'i kaulana no Hawai'i. 'O <u>Mauna Kea</u> ke kuahiwi nani.

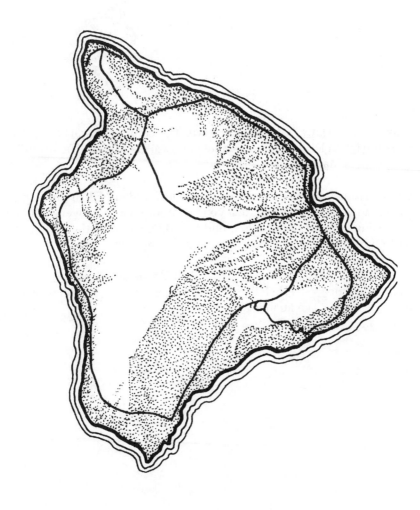

This island is <u>Hawai'i</u>. <u>Hilo</u> is the town. The color o<u>f Hawai'i</u> is <u>red</u>. Its lei is the <u>lehua</u> lei. The famous chief of <u>Hawai'i</u> is <u>Keawe</u>. The beautiful mountain is <u>Mauna Kea</u>.

Can you remember the names, color and lei for Maui? Fill in the blanks; then read your story out loud. If you've forgotten any answers, instead of looking back to Chapter Six, find the Maui story on the CD. Try to write down the Hawaiian words from <u>listening</u> only.

'O <u>Maui</u> kēia mokupuni. 'O _____ ke kūlanakauhale. He _____ ka waiho'olu'u no_____. He lei_____ kona lei. 'O_____ke ali'i kaulana no_____. 'O_____ ke kuahiwi.

Here's a more complicated story about Hawai'i island. Read it as you listen along with the CD several times; then read it out loud. How fluent do you sound?

"O Hawai'i mokupuni ka "mokupuni nui," no ka mea, he nui nō kēlā mokupuni. Ma nā mo'olelo ho'okumu honua o ke au kahiko, 'o Hawai'i ka hiapo o nā mokupuni. 'O Wākea ka makuakāne o Hawai'i mokupuni. 'O Papahānaumoku ka makuahine o Hawai'i mokupuni. Mana'o ka po'e 'epekema, 'o Hawai'i ka mokupuni 'ōpiopio o ka pae 'āina. Wahi a lākou, 'o Kaua'i ka mokupuni kahiko loa o ka pae 'āina. Pololei paha nā mana'o 'elua.

Hawai'i island is the "Big Island," because that island is indeed big. In the creation chants of ancient days, Hawai'i is the first born of the islands. Wākea is the father of Hawai'i island. Papahānaumoku is the mother of Hawai'i island. Scientists think Hawai'i is the youngest island of the chain. According to them, Kaua'i is the oldest island of the chain. Maybe both ideas are right.

d. Mele

This song travels around the island of Hawai'i mentioning names of traditional districts of land, such as Puna, Ka'ū, and Kohala, and the famous sayings that often tell the names of the rain, wind or sea of those places.

Hilo Hanakahi (composer unknown)

Hilo Hanakahi i ka ua Kanilehua
Puna paia 'ala, i ka paia 'ala i ka hala
Ka'ū i ka makani, i ka makani kuehu lepo
Kona i ke kai, i ke kai mā'oki'oki
Kawaihae i ke kai, i ke kai hāwanawana
Waimea i ka ua, i ka ua Kīpu'upu'u
Kohala i ka makani, i ka makani 'Āpa'apa'a
Hāmākua i ka pali, i ka pali lele koa'e
Ha'ina ka puana, 'o Hilo i ka ua Kanilehua.

Conclusion

Aloha hou mai! Pehea ka ʻai ʻana? Ua māʻona? Hello again! How was the Hawaiian "meal" you just finished? Are you full of Hawaiian or did you just have a "light snack"? Do you realize that the five basic sentence patterns we have taught you are the basic patterns used in most spoken Hawaiian? If you know how to use ʻO identification, Aia, He pattern, Action and Description sentences, you should be able to carry on a simple Hawaiian conversation and continue to speak to people as you learn new words.

We hope you enjoyed listening, reading and speaking our beautiful language and that we have "whetted your appetite" for further knowledge. Here in Hawaiʻi there are a variety of Hawaiian language and culture classes being offered through the Department of Education's Adult Night School, Kamehameha Schools Extension Classes, Bishop Museum, the University of Hawaiʻi and community colleges. Local radio and television stations offer programs on Hawaiian language and culture.

If you are outside of Hawaiʻi, there are a number of books and book/CD packages available that can add to your knowledge of Hawaiian. These can be obtained from the publishers listed below.

1. The *Hawaiian Word Book* and CD, illustrated by Robin Yoko Burningham, Bess Press, 1983. Individual words only; good illustrations show meaning. www.besspress.com

2. *Pai Ka Leo,* by ʻAha Pūnana Leo, Bess Press, 1989. Words and music (and cassette tape) for songs sung by the children at the Pūnana Leo Hawaiian language immersion preschool. www.besspress.com

3. *Hawaiian Alphabet*, Pacific Resources for Education and Learning, 2004. Illustrated with children's artwork, the book features 4 or 5 illustrated examples for each letter as well as a word list of English translations. www.besspress.com

4. *Illustrated Hawaiian Dictionary*, Kahikāhealani Wight, illustrated by Robin Yoko Racoma, Bess Press, 1997. New pocket edition includes entries for over 2,500 words, highlighting the most common definitions for each. Thousands of example sentences teach grammar and conversational usage. www.besspress.com

5. *Hawaiian: A Language Map*, Kristine K. Kershul and Lilinoe Andrews, Bilingual Books, Inc. and Bess Press, 2001. An illustrated introduction to over 1,000 Hawaiian words and phrases, categorized by subject, in a portable two-sided folded and laminated format. www.besspress.com

6. *Hawaiian Dictionary*, rev. and enlarged ed., Mary Kawena Puku'i and Samuel H. Elbert, University of Hawai'i Press, 1986. The paperback edition is inexpensive and adequate for beginners. However, serious students of the language will be happier with the more expensive hardcover edition, which includes many more words. www.uhpress.hawaii.edu

7. *Hawaiian Place Names*, Mary Kawena Puku'i, et al., University of Hawai'i Press, 1989. www.uhpress.hawaii.edu

8. *'Ōlelo No'eau.* Mary Kawena Puku'i, et al., Bishop Museum Press, 1983. Hawaiian wise sayings are listed and explained. A challenge for students at all levels of language learning and a touchstone of Hawaiian cultural values. www.bishopmuseum.org/press/press/html

Answer Key

Chapter One

Self-Test 1-1 (p. 3)

Which greeting is correct at each of the times listed below? Choose from **aloha kakahiaka, aloha awakea, aloha ʻauinalā, aloha ahiahi.**

1. 8:10 a.m.	aloha kakahiaka
2. 11:25 a.m.	aloha awakea
3. 1:45 p.m.	aloha awakea
4. 3 p.m.	aloha ʻauinalā
5. 7:13 p.m.	aloha ahiahi
6. 10:50 a.m.	aloha awakea
7. 6:05 p.m.	aloha ahiahi
8. 2:20 p.m.	aloha ʻauinalā
9. 5:30 p.m.	aloha ʻauinalā
10. 9:34 a.m.	aloha kakahiaka
11. 12:04 p.m.	aloha awakea
12. 9:00 p.m.	aloha ahiahi

Self-Test 1-2 (p. 3)

Matching. Write the number of the Hawaiian greeting next to the correct translation.

1. Aloha ahiahi, e Momi.	10. Good noontime everyone.
2. Aloha ʻauinalā.	7. Hello to all of us.
3. Aloha kāua, e koʻu hoaaloha.	1. Good evening, Momi.
4. Aloha kakahiaka kākou.	6. Hello, teacher.
5. Aloha awakea kāua.	8. Good morning, Kainalu.
6. Aloha, e ke kumu.	2. Good afternoon.
7. Aloha kākou.	3. Hello to both of us, my friend.
8. Aloha kakahiaka, e Kainalu.	4. Good morning to all of us.
9. Aloha ahiahi kāua.	5. Good noontime to you and me.
10. Aloha awakea kākou.	9. Good evening to you and me.

Homework 1-1 (p.4)
Translate the following greetings.

1.	Good noontime.	Aloha awakea.
2.	Good morning.	Aloha kakahiaka.
3.	Hello to you and me.	Aloha kāua.
4.	Good evening to us all.	Aloha ahiahi kākou.
5.	Good afternoon to you and me.	Aloha 'auinalā kāua.
6.	Good morning everyone.	Aloha kakahiaka kākou.
7.	Good evening to you and me.	Aloha ahiahi kāua.
8.	Hello everyone.	Aloha kākou.
9.	Good noontime to us all.	Aloha awakea kākou.
10.	Good evening.	Aloha ahiahi.

Self-Test 1-3 (p. 6)
Draw a line from the English pronoun to the Hawaiian translation.

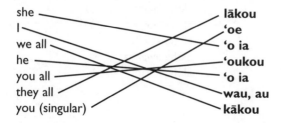

Homework 1-2 (p. 7)

1.	She is sick.	Ma'i **'o ia**.
2.	I am nice.	'Olu'olu **au**.
3.	They are fine.	Maika'i **lākou**.
4.	Mehana, are you happy?	E Mehana, hau'oli **'oe**?
5.	He is tired.	Māluhiluhi **'o ia**.
6.	We all are well.	Maika'i **kākou**.
7.	Yes, I am happy.	'Ae, hau'oli **au**.
8.	You all are kind.	'Olu'olu **'oukou**.
9.	Are they tired?	Māluhiluhi **lākou**?
10.	Is she sick?	Ma'i **'o ia**?

Self-Test 1-4 for ke or ka (p. 8)

1. **ke** kāne	6. **ke** kaikamahine
2. **ka** wahine	7. **ke** ala
3. **ke** aloha	8. **ka** makua
4. **ke** kupuna	9. **ka** imu
5. **ka** hale	10. **ka** 'opihi

Self-Test 1-6 (p. 9)

Matching. Write the number of the English phrase next to its Hawaiian translation.

1. her school	2. kona hale
2. his house	7. ko'u halepule
3. your friend	8. kona* kumu
4. my grandparent	6. kou makuahine
5. her father	10. kona ali'i
6. your mother	4. ko'u kupuna
7. my church	5. kona makuakāne
8. his teacher	9. kou aloha
9. your love	3. kou hoaaloha
10. her chief	1. kona kula

Homework 1-3 (p. 9)

Fill in the blanks with the correct noun announcer.

1. his student	**kona*** haumāna
2. your friend	**kou** hoaaloha
3. that mother	**kēlā** makuahine
4. this store	**kēia** halekū'ai
5. my love	**ko'u** aloha
6. this woman	**kēia** wahine
7. her building	**kona** hale
8. that 'opihi	**kēlā** 'opihi
9. his father	**kona** makuakāne
10. your grandparent	**kou** kupuna

Homework 1-4 (p. 10)

Translate the following phrases into Hawaiian.

1. that school	kēlā kula
2. my church	ko'u halepule
3. this store	kēia halekū'ai
4. her love	kona aloha
5. your husband	kou* kāne
6. the imu	ka imu
7. your teacher	kou* kumu
8. that student	kēlā haumāna
9. his hat	kona pāpale
10. the house	ka hale

Homework 1-5 (p. 10)

Translate the following dialogs from English into Hawaiian.

1. Good evening.	Aloha ahiahi.
Hello to both of us.	Aloha kāua
How are you?	Pehea ʻoe?
I'm tired! How are you?	Māluhiluhi wau! Pehea ʻoe?
I'm fine.	Maikaʻi au.

2. Good afternoon to all of us!	Aloha ʻauinalā kākou!
Yes, good afternoon.	ʻAe, aloha ʻauinalā.
How's school?	Pehea ke kula?
School is fine. We're all happy.	Maikaʻi ke kula. Hauʻoli kākou.
Good! See you later.	Maikaʻi. A hui hou!
Yes. Goodbye 'til we meet again.	ʻAe. Aloha a hui hou.

Chapter Two

Homework 2-3 (p. 22)

Here are words that would like to become **Center** subjects. However, each is incomplete and can't be used as a Center. Complete them so that they can be used. What did you add?

1. ʻo Molokaʻi	7. ʻo Lāʻie
2. ke kaikamahine	8. ke kumu
3. kēia kāne	9. ka imu
4. ʻo Nāihe	10. ʻo Wailau
5. ka halekūʻai	11. ke aloha
6. kona hoaaloha	12. koʻu kupunawahine

Name announcers were added before names. **Noun announcers** were added before nouns. Any noun announcer is correct.

Homework 2-4 (p. 23)

1. Lānaʻi is a name and requires a name announcer (ʻo) before it.
3. Hale is a noun and requires a noun announcer, such as ka or kēlā before it.
5. See # 1.
6. Wrong noun announcer. It should be ka wahine.
10. See # 3.
12. See # 1.

Self-Test 2-3 (p. 23)

Nani nō (o Hāna.)
Liʻiliʻi (kēia halekūʻai)
ʻOluʻolu (o ia.)
ʻOluʻolu (kou halekula?)
Wela nō (kēia lā)

Self-Test 2-4 (p. 23)

1. (Kīlauea) (a place name) is <u>cold</u>.
2. (Your grandmother) is <u>tall</u>.
3. (This island) is <u>pretty</u>.
4. (Mēlia) is <u>slow</u>.
5. (The chief) is <u>smart</u>.

Homework 2-6 (p. 25)

Matching. Write the number of the English sentence next to the correct translation.

1. My mother is strong.
2. Aunty Lehua is little.
3. The carpenter is really sad.
4. Leināʻala is happy.
5. Your house is indeed old.
6. Is that student smart?
7. Her school is famous.
8. That farmer is very tired.
9. Are you well?
10. I'm really sick.

8. Māluhiluhi nō kēlā mahiʻai.
4. Hauʻoli ʻo Leināʻala.
9. Maikaʻi ʻoe?
1. Ikaika koʻu makuahine.
3. Kaumaha nō ke kamanā.
2. Liʻiliʻi ʻo ʻAnakē Lehua.
10. Maʻi nō wau.
5. Kahiko nō kou hale.
7. Kaulana kona kula.
6. Akamai kēlā haumāna?

Now divide the Hawaiian sentences into sections. **Circle** the **Center** subject and **underline** the **Head.**

HEAD	CENTER
<u>Māluhiluhi nō</u>	(kēlā mahiʻai.)
Hauʻoli	ʻo Leināʻala.
Maikaʻi	ʻoe?
Ikaika	koʻu makuahine
Kaumaha nō	ke kamanā.
Liʻiliʻi	ʻo ʻAnakē Lehua.
Maʻi nō	wau.
Kahiko nō	kou hale.
Kaulana	kona kula.
Akamai	kēlā haumāna?

Homework 2-7 (p. 25)

What do these questions and answers say? **Circle** the descriptive word. **Draw a line** between the Head and Center.

1. (Kaulana)| ʻo Kahaʻi?
Is Kahaʻi famous?
2. ʻAe, (Kaulana)| ʻo ia.
Yes, he is famous.
3. (Kaulana)| kona hoaaloha ?
Is her friend famous?
4. ʻAe, (kaulana) nō |kona hoaaloha.
Yes. Her friend is very famous.

5. (Maʻi)| koʻu makuakāne?
Is my father sick?
6. ʻAʻole. (Māluhiluhi)| kou makuakāne.
No. Your father is tired.
7. (Māluhiluhi) | ʻoe?
Are you tired?
8. ʻAʻole (Maikaʻi) | au.
No. Iʻm fine.

Homework 2-8 (p. 25)
Translate the following into Hawaiian.

1. That store is old.
Kahiko kēlā halekūʻai.
2. He is smart.
Akamai ʻo ia.
3. Her friend is nice.
ʻOluʻolu kona hoaaloha.
4. My grandfather is big.
Nui koʻu kupunakāne.
5. The farmer is famous.
Kaulana ka mahiʻai.

6. This fisherman is hot.
Wela kēia lawaʻia.
7. Hilo is cold.
Anuanu ʻo Hilo.
8. Nuʻumealani is tired.
Māluhiluhi ʻo Nuʻumealani.
9. Iʻm sick.
Maʻi au.
10. Your house is pretty!
Nani kou hale!

Self-Test 2-5 (p. 26)

Fill in the blank using **e** or **'o**. Decide whether you are talking <u>to</u> or <u>about</u> the person. Then, translate into English.

<u>E</u> Leialoha, aloha awakea kāua!
Aloha kāua, <u>e</u> ke kaikamahine. Pehea **'o** Nāinoa?
Māluhiluhi **'o** Nāinoa, <u>e</u> Leialoha.
Auē! <u>E</u> ke kaikamahine, pehea 'oe?
Maika'i wau, <u>e</u> Leialoha. Pehea **'o** Kalehua?
Ma'i **'o** Kalehua, <u>e</u> ke kaikamahine,
A hui hou, <u>e</u> Leialoha.
'Ae, aloha a hui hou, <u>e</u> ke kaikamahine.

Leialoha, good noontime to the two of us!
Hello to you and me, girl. How's Nāinoa?
Nāinoa's tired, Leialoha.
Wow! Girl, how are you?
I'm well, Leialoha. How's Kalehua?
Kalehua's sick, girl.
See you later, Leialoha.
Yes, good 'til we meet again, girl.

Homework 2-10 (p. 27)

Draw a line from the Hawaiian to the correct translation.

1. E ke kumu, nāwaliwali 'o Keali'i?   Yes, girl. Lahaina is hot.
2. 'Ae, e ke kaimahine. Wela 'o Lahaina.   Is he smart, my friend?
3. 'A'ole. Maikai nō 'o Keali'i e ke keiki.   Namau'u, how is Melelani?
4. Akamai 'o ia, e ko'u hoaaloha?   Fisherman, is Uluwehi poor?
5. 'Ae. 'Eleu kēlā kāne, e ka wahine.   Teacher, is Keali'i weak?
6. E Nāmau'u, pehea 'o Melelani?   Yes, that man is lively, lady.
7. Hau'oli ko'u* pōpoki, e Kau'i.   No. Keali'i is very well, boy.
8. E ka lawai'a, 'ilihune 'o Uiuwehi?   My cat is happy, Kau'i.

Homework 2-11 (p. 27)
Translate the following into Hawaiian.

1. How is Maui, Kainoa?   Pehea ʻo Maui, e Kainoa?
2. Maui is pretty, my friend.   Nani ʻo Maui, e koʻu hoaaloha.
3. Grandmother, is Leilehua sick? E ke kupunawahine, maʻi ʻo Leilehua?
4. Yes, Makana. Leilehua is sick. ʻAe, e Makana. Maʻi ʻo Leilehua.
5. No, Makana. Leilehua is well.   ʻAʻole, e Makana. Maikaʻi ʻo Leilehua.

Homework 2-12 (p. 28)

Translate the following dialogs into Hawaiian.

1. Good evening lady.   Aloha ahiahi, e ka wahine.
   Good evening. How are you?   Aloha ahiahi. Pehea ʻoe?
   I'm really tired. See you later. Māuhiluhi nō au. A hui hou.
   Yes, goodbye.   ʻAe. A hui hou aku nō.

2. Hello to both of us, teacher.   Aloha kāua, e ke kumu.
   Good morning, Kuʻulei.   Aloha kakahiaka, e Kuʻulei.
   How's the student?   Pehea ka haumāna?
   She's fine, thanks.   Maikaʻi ʻo ia, mahalo.

3. Father (formal), hello.   E ka makuakāne, aloha.
   Hello, Mokihana.   Aloha, e Mokihana.
   How's the store?   Pehea ka halekūʻai?
   The store is fine.   Maikaʻi ka halekūʻai.
   Are you happy?   Hauʻoli ʻoe?
   Yes, I'm really happy.   ʻAe. Hauʻoli nō au.

Chapter Three

Self-Test 3-1 (p. 38)

Translate the following phrases.

1. your name kou inoa	5. my car koʻu kaʻa	9. your friend kou hoaaloha
2. his house kona hale	6. his name kona inoa	10. her name kona inoa
3. her store kona halekūʻai	7. your father kou makuakāne	11. his mother kona makuahine
4. my name koʻu inoa	8. her church kona halepule	12. my husband koʻu* kane

Homework 3-1 (p. 38)

Matching. Write the number of the Hawaiian sentence next to the correct English translation. Read the Hawaiian out loud.

1. **ʻO wai kona inoa?**
2. **ʻO Niuliʻi koʻu inoa.**
3. **ʻO wai koʻu inoa?**
4. **ʻO Kealiʻi koʻu inoa?**
5. **ʻO Makanani kou inoa.**
6. **ʻO wai kou inoa?**
7. **ʻO Waiʻolu kona inoa.**
8. **ʻO Niuliʻi kou inoa?**
9. **ʻO Heanu koʻu inoa.**
10. **ʻO Kealiʻi kou inoa.**

6. What's your name?
5. Makanani is your name.
7. Waiʻolu is her name.
2. Niuliʻi is my name.
1. What's her name?
9. Heanu is my name.
10. Kealiʻi is your name.
3. What is my name?
4. Is Kealiʻi my name?
8. Is Niuliʻi your name?

Homework 3-2 (p. 38)

Fill in the blank with the correct possessive pronoun.

What is her name?	**'O wai** <u>kona</u> **inoa?**
Her name is Lehua.	**'O Lehua** <u>kona</u> **inoa.**
What's your name?	**'O wai** <u>kou</u> **inoa?**
My name is Kāwika.	**'O Kāwika** <u>ko'u</u> **inoa.**
What's my name, Mother?	**'O wai** <u>ko'u</u> inoa, **e ka makuahine?**
Your name is Keikilani.	**'O Keikilani** <u>kou</u> **inoa.**
Ku'ulei, what's his name?	**E Ku'ulei,** 'o wai <u>kona</u> **inoa?**
His name is Nohea.	**'O Nohea** <u>kona</u> **inoa.**

Homework 3-3 (p. 39)

Translate the following pairs of questions and answers into Hawaiian.

1. What is his name?
'O wai kona inoa?

His name is Kamanu.
'O Kamanu kona inoa.

2. What's your name?
'O wai kou inoa?

My name is Melelani.
'O Melelani ko'u inoa.

3. Melelani is your name.
'O Melelani kou inoa.

Is your name Kamanu?
'O Kamanu kou inoa?

4. No, my name is Kawehiokekai.
'A'ole, 'o Kawehiokekai ko'u inoa.

Hello, Kawehiokekai.
Aloha, e Kawehiokekai.

5. Melelani, what's my name?
E Melelani, 'o wai ko'u inoa?

Your name is Nāmaka.
'O Nāmaka kou inoa.

6. Is Nāmaka my name?
'O Nāmaka ko'u inoa?

Yes, Nāmaka is my name.
'Ae, 'o Nāmaka ko'u inoa.

7. What is her name, sir (man)?
'O wai kona inoa, e ke kāne?

Her name is Nani, lady.
'O Nani kona inoa, e ka wahine.

8. Father, is your name Hau'olimau?
E ka makuakāne, 'o Hau'olimau kou inoa?

No, my name is Hau'olikeola.
'A'ole, 'o Hau'olikeola ko'u inoa.

Self-Test 3-2 (p. 40)

Translate the following into Hawaiian.

1. Who's that?
   'O wai kēlā?
2. Who is the teacher?
   'O wai ke kumu?
3. Who are you?
   'O wai 'oe?
4. Who is that man?
   'O wai kēlā kāne?
5. Who is she?
   'O wai 'o ia?

6. Who is this child?
   'O wai kēia keiki?
7. Who is Kāwika?
   'O wai 'o Kāwika?
8. Who's my friend?
   'O wai ko'u hoaaloha?
9. Who's your father?
   'O wai kou makuakāne?
10. Who are we (all)?
    'O wai kākou?

Chapter Four

Self-Test 4-3 (p. 50)

Circle the Center in the following sentences. Underline the Head. Then translate into English.

1. He lawai'a (ke kāpena.)   The captain is a fisherman.
2. He Hawai'i (au.)   I am (a) Hawaiian.
3. He i'a (ka mahimahi.)   Mahimahi is a fish.
4. He malihini ('oe.)   You are a newcomer.
5. He haumāna ('o Noenoe.)   Noenoe is a student.
6. He haleleka (kēlā hale nui?)   Is that large building a post office?
7. He kupunakāne (kēia māka'i.)   This police officer is a grandfather.
8. He 'ohana nui (lākou.)   They are a large family.
9. He 'āina ua ('o Mānoa?)   Is Mānoa a rainy land?
10. He makuahine ('o ia?)   Is she a mother?

Homework 4-1 (p.52)

Matching. Write the number of the Hawaiian sentence next to its English translation.

1. He aha kou* lawaiʻa?	5. Her friend is a Japanese.
2. He Pukikī ʻo ia.	4. My dog is a spaniel.
3. He kupuna kēia kāne.	8. What is this person?
4. He spaniel koʻu* ʻīlio.	7. What is that teacher?
5. He Kepanī kona hoaaloha.	2. Heʻs a Portuguese.
6. He kinai ahi koʻu makuakāne.	1. What is your fisherman?
7. He aha kēlā kumu?	9. That teacher is a farmer.
8. He aha kēlā kanaka?	10. The building is a hospital.
9. He mahiʻai kēlā kumu.	6. My father is a firefighter.
10. He haukapila ka hale.	3. This man is a grandparent.

Homework 4-2 (p. 52)

Translate the following sentences into Hawaiian.

1. What is her friend?	He aha kona hoaaloha?
2. Her friend is a Hawaiian.	He Hawaiʻi kona hoaaloha.
3. What is the homework?	He aha ka haʻawina?
4. A book is the homework.	He puke ka haʻawina.
5. What is this commoner?	He aha kēia makaʻāinana?
6. This commoner is a farmer.	He mahiʻai kēia makaʻāinana.
7. What is the police officer?	He aha ka mākaʻi?
8. The police officer is a grandmother.	He kupunawahine ka mākaʻi.
9. What is your baby?	He aha kou* pēpē?
10. My baby is a boy.	He keikikāne koʻu* pēpē.

Chapter Five

Homework 5-3 (p. 63)

Translate the following into Hawaiian.

1. This doctor works.
   Hana kēia kauka.
2. Kuʻupuni asks.
   Nīnau ʻo Kuʻupuni.
3. I go.
   Hele au.
4. The student answers.
   Pane ka haumāna.
5. That chief leads.
   Alakaʻi kēiā aliʻi.

6. We all eat.
   ʻAi kākou.
7. Her minister sits.
   Noho kona *kahunapule.
8. This fisherman sees.
   ʻIke kēia lawaiʻa.
9. Nāinoa plays.
   Pāʻani ʻo Nāinoa.
10. You speak the Hawaiian language.
    ʻŌlelo ʻoe i ka ʻōlelo Hawaiʻi.

Homework 5-4 (p. 64)

Matching. Write the number of the Hawaiian sentence next to its English translation.

1. Ua mākaʻikaʻi ʻo Kanalu i kēia kakahiaka.
2. E nīnau ana lākou i ka mākaʻi.
3. Ke noho nei koʻu* ʻīlio i koʻu kaʻa.
4. Kūʻai aku kēiā kāne i ka ʻāina.

5. E ʻauʻau ana ʻoukou i kēia lā?
6. Ke inu nei ke kinai ahi?
7. Ua pāʻani kou* papa i ke kakahiaka.

8. ʻŌlelo ke kupunakāne i ke kīwī.

4. That man sells land.
3. My dog is sitting in my car.
6. Is the firefighter drinking?
7. Your class played in the morning.
2. They will ask the police officer.
5. Will you all swim today?
8. The grandfather speaks on the TV.
1. Kanalu went sightseeing this morning.

Homework 5-6 (p. 65)

Translate the following sentences. Color the **Heads** yellow and the **Centers** orange. Remember, some **Heads** will not contain any verb tense markers.

1. My friend sits.	Noho koʻu hoaaloha.
2. This boy is eating.	Ke ʻai nei kēia keikikāne.
3. She will read.	E heluhelu ana ʻo ia.
4. The farmer ate.	Ua ʻai ka mahiʻai.
5. Nālei is answering.	Ke pane nei ʻo Nālei.
6. The doctor will stand.	E kū ana ke kauka.
7. Her cat ran.	Ua holo kona* pōpoki.
8. That granddaughter played.	Ua pāʻani kēlā moʻopunawahine.
9. They all are sightseeing.	Ke mākaʻikaʻi nei lākou.
10. Momi spoke.	Ua ʻōlelo ʻo Momi.

Homework 5-8 (p.66)

Complete the **Tail** section in these Hawaiian sentences. Follow the English translation.

1. You work <u>at the hospital</u>.	Hana ʻoe **i ka haukapila**.
2. Kanani sits <u>at the shopping center</u>.	Noho ʻo Kanani **i ke kikowaenakūʻai**.
3. The man looks <u>at his hand</u>.	Nānā ke kāne **i kona lima**.
4. She eats <u>the poi</u>.	ʻAi ʻo ia **i ka poi**.
5. That girl prays <u>in the morning</u>.	Pule kēlā kaikamahine **i ke kakahiaka**.
6. Keola runs <u>to the hotel</u>.	Holo ʻo Keola **i ka hōkele**.
7. His cousin sings <u>that song</u>.	Hīmeni kona hoahānau **i kēlā mele**.
8. I drink <u>this water</u>.	Inu wau **i kēia wai**.
9. Winona lives <u>on this island</u>.	Noho ʻo Winona i **kēia mokupuni**.
10. My boy plays <u>at the party</u>.	Pāʻani koʻu* keikikāne **i ka pāʻina**.

Homework 5-9 (p. 67)

Draw a circle around the **Center** in the Hawaiian sentences above.
Underline the **Head**. Draw a line through the **Tail**. Now color the
Center orange, the Head yellow, the Tail brown.

1. You work <u>at the hospital</u>.	Hana (oe) ~~ika haukapila~~.
2. Kanani sits <u>at the shopping center</u>.	Noho (ʻo Kanani) ~~i ke kikowaenakūʻai~~.
3. The man looks <u>at his hand</u>.	Nānā (ke kāne) ~~i kona lima~~.
4. She eats <u>the poi</u>.	ʻAi (o ia) ~~i ka poi~~.
5. That girl prays <u>in the morning</u>.	Pule (kēlā kaikamahine) ~~i ke kakahiaka~~.
6. Keola runs <u>to the hotel</u>.	Holo (ʻo Keola) ~~i ka hōkele~~.
7. His cousin sings <u>that song</u>.	Himeni (kona hoahānau) ~~i kēlā mele~~.
8. I drink <u>this water</u>.	Inu (wau) ~~i kēia wai~~.
9. Winona lives <u>on this island</u>.	Noho (ʻo Winona) ~~i kēia mokupuni~~.
10. My boy plays <u>at the party</u>.	Pāʻani (koʻu* keikikāne) ~~i ka pāʻina~~.

Homework 5-10 (p. 67)

Translate the following into Hawaiian. Remember that the **Tail
announcer** is always needed, even though it may not be indicated by
the English sentence.

1. This lady works at the store.	Hana kēia wahine i ka halekūʻai.
2. Kōnane sees the mountain.	ʻIke ʻo Kōnane i ke kuahiwi.
3. The captain sings on the ship.	Hīmeni ke kāpena i ka mokuahi.
4. She drinks in the afternoon.	Inu ʻo ia i ka ʻauinalā.
5. Do you take a bath on Saturday?	ʻAuʻau ʻoe i ka pōʻaono?

Chapter Six

Homework 6-2 (p. 80)

Matching. Write the number of the Hawaiian phrase next to its English translation.

1. kēia mau pālule aloha	5. the lanterns
2. nā pākaukau	6. his parents
3. koʻu mau hoahānau	1. these aloha shirts
4. kēlā mau pahi	8. your guava trees
5. nā kukuihelepō	9. the post offices
6. kona mau mākua	10. those little fishes
7. kēia mau pūpū	4. those knives
8. kou* mau kumukuawa	2. the tables
9. na haleleka	3. my cousins
10. kēlā mau iʻa liʻiliʻi	7. these shells

Homework 6-3 (p. 80)

Pluralize the following noun announcer plus noun phrases. Translate the pluralized phrase into English.

1. kēia mau makahiki	these years
2. nā holoholona	the animals
3. kou* mau hoe	your paddles
4. kēlā mau papa heʻenalu	those surfboards
5. nā kāhunapule	the ministers
6. kēia mau pō	these nights
7. kona* mau kālā	his dollars
8. nā ʻilio	the dogs
9. koʻu mau lā hānau	my birthdays
10. nā kamaʻāina	the local people

Homework 6-5 (p. 81)

Matching. Write the number of the Hawaiian sentence next to the correct translation.

1. Aia kēia keiki i ke kahua pāʻani.	6. No. The car is on the street.
2. Aia ʻo ia i kona halekūʻai.	7. Where's my comb?
3. Aia ʻo Momi i ʻaneʻi.	10. Yes. He's at work.
4. Aia ka hālāwai i ka hola ʻeono.	1. This child is on the playground.
5. Aia ke kaʻa i ka halekaʻa?	9. Is Palani at work?
6. ʻAʻole. Aia ke kaʻa i ke alanui.	2. She's at her store.
7. Aia i hea koʻu* kahi?	4. The meeting is at six o'clock.
8. Aia kou* kahi i ka pākaukau.	3. Momi's here.
9. Aia ʻo Palani i ka hana?	5. Is the car in the garage?
10. ʻAe. Aia ʻo ia i ka hana.	8. Your comb is on the table.

Homework 6-6 (p. 82)

Translate the following sentences into Hawaiian.

1. His son is at school.
   Aia kona* keikikāne i ke kula.

2. Kanoni is in her bedroom.
   Aia ʻo Kanoni i kona lumimoe.

3. That plumeria is in my lei.
   Aia kēlā puamēlia i koʻu lei.

4. Is that plumeria in my lei?
   Aia kēlā puamēlia i koʻu lei?

5. The test is at church.
   Aia ka hoʻike i ka halepule.

6. You are in my house!
   Aia ʻoe i koʻu hale!

7. Is the class this evening?
   Aia ka papa i kēia ahiahi

8. No. The class is this noontime.
   ʻAʻole. Aia ka papa i kēia awakea.

9. Hulali is at the post office.
   Aia ʻo Hulali i ka haleleka.

10. This cat is on your leg.
    Aia kēia pōpoki i kou wāwae.

Chapter Seven

Homework 7-1 (p. 94)

Matching. Write the number of the Hawaiian sentence next to its English translation.

1. 'O Maile kou makuahine.
2. 'O kēia hale 'aina 'o ka Willows.
3. 'O kēlā mea he'enalu ka mea akamai.
4. 'O ka wai 'alani ka mea inu?
5. 'O kēia uala kona* 'aina awakea.
6. 'O ka noho 'olu'olu kēia.
7. 'O Beretania ke alanui kaulana.
8. 'O kona* lēkiō kēlā lēkiō.
9. 'O Pu'uloa 'o Pearl Harbor.
10. 'O ka mahi'ai kona* hana.

8. That radio is his radio.
9. Pearl Harbor is Pu'uloa.**
6. This is the comfortable chair.
10. His work is farming.
2. The Willows is this restaurant.
3. The smart one is that surfer.
1. Your mother is Maile.
5. Her lunch is this sweet potato.
4. Is the drink orange juice?
7. The famous street is Beretania.

** Pu'uloa is the Hawaiian name for Pearl Harbor.

Homework 7-2 (p. 94)

Translate the following sentence with the **'O identification** pattern.

1. That woman is the teacher.
2. This is your job.
3. I am the newcomer.
4. Nā'ala is that strong captain.
5. Is Nā'ala that strong captain?
6. The poi is his food.
7. That is the pretty lei.
8. She is my mother.
9. You are her grandfather.
10. Nāihe is the ali'i today.

'O ke kumu kēlā wahine.
'O kou* hana kēia.
'O ka malihini au.
'O kēlā kāpena ikaika 'o Nā'ala.
'O kēlā kāpena ikaika 'o Nā'ala?
'O kona* mea 'ai ka poi.
'O ka lei nani kēlā.
'O ko'u makuahine 'o ia.
'O kona kupunakāne 'oe.
'O ke ali'i 'o Nāihe i kēia la.

Homework 7-3 (p. 96)

Matching. Write the number of the Hawaiian command next to its translation.

1. E hāpai i ka 'ōpala!
2. Mai nānā aku i ke kiwi!
3. E hānai i nā 'īlio i kēia 'auinalā!
4. Mai 'aihue i knoa ka'a!
5. Mai 'aka'aka aku i kou hoahānau!
6. E kama'ilio i ke kumu!
7. Mai uē, e ka pēpē!

5. Don't laugh at your cousin!
3. Feed the dogs this afternoon!
1. Carry the garbage!
2. Don't watch TV!
7. Don't cry, baby!
6. Don't talk to the teacher!
4. Don't steal her car!

Hawaiian-English Glossary

A

'a'ala	sweet-smelling, fragrant
'ae	yes
'aha	gathering
aheahe	gentle (breeze)
ahi	fire
ahiahi	evening
'ai	food, taro, to eat
'aihue	thief, to steal
'aina	meal
'aina ahiahi	dinner
'aina awakea	lunch
'aina kakahiaka	breakfast
'āina	land
'aka'aka	laugh, to laugh
'ākala	pink
akamai	clever, smart
aku	directional: away from speaker
akua	god
ala	pathway, to wake up
alahele	pathway, trail
alaka'i	leader, to lead
'alani	orange
alanui	road
ali'i	royalty, chief/chiefess
aloha	love
ana	cave
'ane'i	here (location)
'ano	type, kind
anuanu	cold
ao	day, light, consciousness
'ao'ao	side, page
'a'ole	no, negation
'apōpō	tomorrow
au	time, current
'au'au	to swim, bathe
'aumakua	family guardian
awakea	noontime
awāwa	valley
'āwīwī	quickly

E

e	vocative (hey) used when addressing someone
'ē	strange, foreign
'eha	sore, painful
'ehā	four
'ehiku	seven
'eiwa	nine
'ekahi	one
'ekolu	three
'ele'ele	black
'eleu	lively, spirited
'elima	five
'elua	two
emi	cheap, inexpensive
'eono	six
'epekema	science, scientist

H

ha'aha'a	humility, humble
ha'aheo	pride, proud
ha'alele	to leave
hā'awi	to give
ha'awina	lesson, homework
hahai	to follow
hala	pass by, pass away
hālau	canoe shed, hula school
hale	building, house
hale 'aina	restaurant
halekula	schoolhouse
halekū'ai	store
haleleka	post office
halemāka'i	police station
halepule	church
hāmama	opened
hana	work, activity, to work, to do activity
hānai	to feed, raise animals, children; to adopt
hānau	to give birth
hanohano	distinguished, honored
hao	metal, to blast, smite
haumāna	student
hau'oli	happy
hāwanawana	whisper, to whisper
he'e	octopus, to slide around like an octopus

he'enalu	to surf
hele	to go
hele mai	to come
helu	number, to count
heluhelu	to read
hemahema	awkward
hemolele	pure, pristine
hewa	mistake, wrong
hiamoe	to sleep
hiapo	first-born child
hiki	to be able to, to arrive
hilahila	embarrassed, ashamed, shy
hīmeni	to sing
hinahina	grey
hoaaloha	friend
hō'ailona	sign, symbol
hoe	paddle, to paddle
hohono	bad-smelling (body odor)
ho'i	to return, to go back home
ho'i mai	to come back
hō'ike	show, demonstration, to demonstrate, reveal
hōkele	hotel
holo	to run, move around
holoi	to wash
holoholona	animal
honi	kiss, to kiss, to smell
honua	earth
ho'olohe	to listen
ho'oponopono	to fix, repair, correct
ho'opunipuni	to lie
hou	new, again
hui	group, to meet
hula	dance (hula), to dance

I

i'a	fish
'ike	knowledge, to see
ikaika	strong
'ilihune	poor
'īlio	dog
'ino	evil, bad, storm
inoa	name
inu	to drink

'iole   rat, mouse

K

ka	the
ka'a	car
kahakai	beach
kahiko	old
kahua	field, flat plain
kahuna	expert, priest
kahunapule	minister
kai	sea
kaikamahine	girl, daughter
kakahiaka	morning
kākau	to write
kākou	all of us
kālā	money
kalaka	truck
kalaunu	crown
kali	to wait
kalo	taro
kāma'a	shoes
kama'āina	local person
kama'ilio	to converse
kanaka	human being
kāne	man, husband
kanu	to plant
kapa	tapa, blanket
kapikala	capital
kapua'i	foot (measurement)
kāpulu	messy
kāua	you and I
kaua	war, battle, to make war
kauka	doctor
kaulana	famous
kaumaha	heavy, sad
kauoha	command, order, to order, command
ke	the
kēia	this
keiki	child
keikikāne	boy
kēlā	that
kelepona	telephone, to telephone
kena	quenched (thirst)

keʻokeʻo	white
kiaʻāina	state governor
kiʻekiʻe	tall, high
kiʻi	drawing, image, to go get something
kikiki	ticket
kikowaenakūʻai	shopping center
kilakila	majestic
kinai	to extinguish fire
kino	body
kipa	to visit
kīwī	T.V.
koa	soldier, courageous
kokoke	close to (distance)
kōkua	help, to help
kolohe	mischievous
komo	to enter
kona	his, her
kopalā	shovel
kou	your
koʻu	my
kū	to stop, appear
kua	back
kūʻai aku	to sell
kūʻai mai	to buy
kuahiwi	mountain
kuehu	to stir up (dust), to shake
kuene	waiter/waitress, steward/stewardess
kūkulu	to build
kula	school
kūlanakauhale	town, city
kula nui	university
kumu	teacher, source
kumukūʻai	price
kumulāʻau	tree
kumupuakenikeni	puakenikeni tree
kūpono	appropriate, proper
kupuna	grandparent
kupunakāne	grandfather
kupunawahine	grandmother

L

lā	day, sun
lae	forehead, peninsula

laila	there (aforementioned place)
lani	noble, chief
lāpule	Sunday
lauhala	leaf of hala tree, products made from this leaf
lawa	enough
lawai'a	fisherman, to fish
lawe aku	to take
lawe mai	to bring
lei	garland, necklace
lēkiō	radio
lele	to jump
lepo	dirt, dirty
like	like
lima	arm, hand
limu	seaweed
lohi	slow
lō'ihi	long
lole	clothes
lolouila	computer
lumi	room
luna	on top, above

M

ma'alahi	easy
mae	wilted
ma'ema'e	clean
mahalo	thanks, gratitude
maha'oi	too aggressive, too bold
mahi'ai	farmer, to farm
mahina	moon, month
mai	directional: toward speaker
ma'i	sick, ill
mai'a	banana
maika'i	good, fine, well
maka	eye
maka'āinana	commoner
makaaniani	eyeglasses
makahiki	year
māka'i	police officer
māka'ika'i	tourist, to tour, sightsee
makana	gift
makani	wind
maka'u	afraid, dangerous

mākaukau	prepared, ready
make	dead
makewai	thirsty
makua	parent
makuahine	mother
makuakāne	father
māla	garden
mālama	to take care of, keep
mālie	calm
malihini	newcomer
māluhiluhi	tired
mamao	distance, distant, far
mana	spiritual power
mana'o	thought, opinion, to think
mā'ona	full stomach, satiated
maopopo	understood, understand
mau	pluralizer
mea	thing, person
meakanu	plant
mele	song
melemele	yellow
moana	deep ocean
mokulele	airplane
mokupuni	island
moloā	lazy
momona	fat, sweet-tasting
mo'olelo	story, history
mo'opuna	grandchild
mo'opunakāne	grandson
mo'opunawahine	granddaughter
mua	before, first
muliloa	last-born child

N

na'auao	wise, educated
nalu	wave
nānā	to watch, observe
nani	pretty
nāwaliwali	weak
nehinei	yesterday
nīele	nosy
nīnau	question, to ask a question
no	for, about

nō	really, indeed, truly
no'eau	skilled, clever
noho	chair, to sit, to live someplace
nui	big

O

'ō	spear, over there (location)
'o ia	he/she
'oe	you
'ohana	family
'ōlelo	language, speech
'ōlelo no'eau	wise saying
ola	life, health
'olu'olu	kind, comfortable
'ōma'oma'o	green
one	sand
'ono	delicious
o'o	mature
'ōpala	garbage
'ōpū	stomach

P

pā hale	house lot, yard
pa'a	stuck, completed, firm
pa'akiki	difficult
pā'ani	game, play, to play
pae 'āina	island chain, archipelago
paia	wall
pā'ina	party
pākaukau	desk, table
pali	cliff
pane	answer, to answer
pani	to close
papa	class
papa he'enalu	surfboard
pāpale	hat
pau	finished, destroyed
pehea	how
pepa	paper
pēpē	baby
piholo	to sink, drown
pili	close proximity or close relationship
pilikia	trouble, problem

pipiʻi	expensive
pō	darkness, night, ignorance
pōʻahā	Thursday
pōʻakahi	Monday
pōʻakolu	Wednesday
pōʻalima	Friday
pōʻalua	Tuesday
pōʻaono	Saturday
poʻi	to break (waves)
pōʻino	storm
pōkole	short
pololei	correct, right, straight
pōloli	hungry
poni	purple
pono	proper
poʻo	head
poʻokela	champion
pōpoki	cat
pua	flower
puana	refrain (song)
puke	book
pule	week, prayer
puni	encircle, go around
pūpū	shell
pupuka	ugly
puʻuwai	heart

U

ua	rain
uaki	watch, clock
uē	to cry
ʻuhane	spirit, soul
uʻi	beautiful
uila	lightning, electricity
ulana	to weave
ʻulaʻula	red
uliuii	dark blue
ulu kukui	kukui grove

W

wā	time period, era
waʻa	canoe
wahine	woman

wai	water
waihoʻoluʻu	color
waiwai	rich
wānana	to foretell, predict
wāwae	leg, foot
wehe	to open, remove, take off
wela	hot
wikiwiki	quick, fast
wīwī	thin

English-Hawaiian Glossary

A

able to, can	hiki
adornment	wehi, kāhiko
afraid	makaʻu
airplane	mokulele
animal	holoholona
answer	pane
appropriate	kūpono
archipelago	paeʻāina
awake, to awaken	ala
awkward	hemahema

B

baby	pēpē
back	kua
bad	ʻino
bad-smelling	hohono
banana	maiʻa
beach	kahakai
beautiful	uʻi, nani
bed	moe
bedroom	lumimoe
Bible	Paipala
big	nui
bird	manu
birth, to give birth	hānau
birthday	lā hānau
black	ʻeleʻele
blanket	kapa
boat (steamship)	mokuahi
book	puke
boy	keikikāne
breakfast	ʻaina kakahiaka
bring	lawe mai
build	kūkulu
building	hale
bury	kanu
buy	kūʻai mai

C

calico	kalakoa
calm	mālie
canoe	wa'a
canoe shed	hālau
capital	kapikala
captain	kāpena
car	ka'a
cat	pōpoki
cave	ana
chair	noho
child	keiki
church	halepule
class	papa
clean (adj.)	ma'ema'e
to clean	ho'oma'ema'e
cliff	pali
climb, rise up	pi'i
clock	uaki
close (distance)	kokoke
close (relationship)	pili
coffee	kope
color	waiho'olu'u
comb	kahi
come	hele mai
come back	ho'i mai
comfortable	'olu'olu
command	kauoha
commoner	maka'āinana
computer	lolouila
converse	kama'ilio
correct	pololei
count	helu
courageous	koa
create	ho'okumu
creation of world	ho'okumu honua
cry	uē

D

dance	hula
darkness	pō
daughter	kaikamahine
day, sun	lā

daylight, daytime	ao
dead	make
delicious	'ono
demonstrate, demonstration	hō'ike
desire	'i'ini, makemake
desk	pākaukau
die	hala
difficult	pa'akikī
dinner	'aina ahiahi
dirty	lepo
distinguished	hanohano
doctor	kauka
dog	'īlio
dolphin	nai'a
draw, drawing	ki'i
to drink	inu
drink	mea inu
drown	piholo

E

ear	pepeiao
earth	honua
easy	ma'alahi
embarrassed	hilahila
English language	'ōlelo Haole
enough	lawa
enter	komo
era, time period	wā
expensive	pipi'i
eye	maka

F

family	'ohana
famous	kaulana
far	mamao
farmer	mahi'ai
fast	'āwīwī, wikiwiki
fat	momona
father	makuakāne
feed	hānai
fence	pā
field	kahua
finished	pau

firefighter	kinai ahi
fish	iʻa
fisherman	lawaiʻa
flower	pua
follow	hāhai
food	mea ʻai
foot	wāwae
forehead	lae
four	ʻehā
fragrance	ʻala
Friday	pōʻalima
friend	hoaaloha
front	alo
fruit	hua ʻai
fruit juice	wai hua ʻai
full (of liquid)	piha
full (of food), satiated	māʻona

G

garden	māla
gather	ʻohi
genesis	kinohi
gentle (breeze)	aheahe
gift	makana
girl	kaikamahine
give	hāʻawi
glasses (eye)	makaaniani
go	hele
god	akua
good	maikaʻi
governor	kiaʻāina
grab	hopu
grandchild	moʻopuna
granddaughter	moʻopunawahine
grandfather	kupunakāne
grandmother	kupunawahine
grandparent	kupuna
grandson	moʻopunakāne
grave	he
green	ʻōmaʻomaʻo
grey	hinahina
group	hui

H

happy	hau'oli
harm	hana'ino
hat	pāpale
he	'o ia
head	po'o
healthy	ola
hear	ho'olohe
heart	pu'uwai
heavy	kaumaha
help	kōkua
here (location)	'ane'i
hole	lua
hospital	haukapila
hot	wela
hotel	hōkele
hour	hola
house	hale
hula school	hālau
human	kanaka
humble	ha'aha'a
hungry	pōloli
husband	kāne

I

ill	ma'i
inexpensive	emi
island	mokupuni

J

Japanese	Kepanī
job, activity	hana
jump	lele

K

kind (nice)	'olu'olu
kind (type, brand)	'ano
kiss	honi
knowledge, to know	ike

L

land	'āina
language	'ōlelo

last-born child	muliloa
laugh	'aka'aka
lazy	moloā
lead, leader	alaka'i
learn	a'o mai
leave	ha'alele
lie, tell a lie	ho'opunipuni
lie down	moe
life	ola
lifestyle	nohona
listen	ho'olohe
live someplace	noho
lively	'eleu
local person	kama'āina
lonely	mehameha
long	lō'ihi
love	aloha

M

majestic	kilakila
man	kāne
market	mākeke
mature	o'o
meal	'aina
meat	'i'o
meeting	hālāwai
messy	kāpulu
metal	hao
minister	kahunapule
mischievous	kolohe
mist	hune, 'ehu
mistake	hewa
Monday	pō'akahi
money	kālā
month	mahina, malama
moon	mahina
morning	kakahiaka
mountain	kuahiwi, mauna
my	ko'u, ka'u

N

name	inoa
nationality	lāhui

new	hou
newcomer	malihini
newspaper	nūpepa
night	pō
nine	'eiwa
noble	ali'i
noontime	awakea
nosy	nīele
number	helu

O

octopus	he'e
old	kahiko
open	wehe
opened	hāmama
orange	'alani

P

paddle, to paddle	hoe
painful	'eha
paper	pepa
parent	makua
party	pā'ina
pass by, pass away	hala
pathway	alahele
peninsula, point	lae
people	po'e, kanaka
picture	ki'i
pig	pua'a
pink	'ākala
plant	meakanu
to plant	kanu
play, to play	pā'ani
police	māka'i
police station	halemāka'i
poor	'ilihune
post office	haleleka
prayer, to pray	pule
predict	wānana
prepared	mākaukau
pretty	nani
price	kumukū'i
pride, proud	ha'aheo

problem	pilikia
proper	kūpono
protect	ho'omalu, kia'i
pure, pristine	hemolele
purple	poni

Q

quenched thirst	kena
question	nīnau
quick	'āwīwī

R

radio	lēkiō
rain	ua
rat	'iole
read	heluhelu
refrain (song)	puana
religious site	heiau
repair	ho'oponopono
restaurant	hale 'aina
return, go back	ho'i
rice	laiki
rich	waiwai
road, street	alanui
rock	pōhaku
room	lumi
run	holo

S

sad	kaumaha
sale	ku'aiemi
sand	one
Saturday	pō'aono
school	kula
schoolhouse	halekula
sea	kai
seaweed	limu
to see, sight	'ike
she	'o ia
shell	pūpū
shirt	pālule
shoe, shoes	kāma'a
short	pōkole

shovel	kopalā
side	ʻaoʻao
sign, symbol	hōʻailona
silence	hāmau
sing, song	hīmeni, mele
six	ʻeono
skilled	noʻeau, mākaukau
slow	lohi
smart	akamai
smell	honi
son	keikikāne
soul, spirit	ʻuhane
spiritual power	mana
steal, thief	ʻaihue
stir up (dust)	kuehu
stomach	ʻōpū
store	halekūʻai
storm	pōʻino
story	moʻolelo
strange	ʻa no ʻē
strong	ikaika
student	haumāna
sun	lā
Sunday	lāpule
to surf	heʻenalu
surfboard	papa heʻenalu
sweet-tasting	momona
sweetheart	ipo
swim	ʻauʻau, ʻau

T

take	lawe aku
take care of	mālama
take off, remove	wehe
tall	lōʻihi, kiʻekiʻe
taro	kalo
teacher	kumu
telephone	kelepona
television	kīwī
thanks	mahalo
that	kēlā
the	ka, ke
there	laila (already know name of place)

thief	ʻaihue
thin	wīwī
thirsty	makewai
this	kēia
thought, to think	manaʻo
three	ʻekolu
Thursday	pōʻahā
ticket	kikiki
time	manawa
tired	māluhiluhi
tomorrow	lā ʻapōpō
tour, tourist	mākaʻikaʻi
towel, to dry	kāwele
town	kūlanakauhale
trouble	pilikia
truck	kalaka
Tuesday	pōʻalua
two	ʻelua

U

ugly	pupuka
understand, understood	maopopo
university	kula nui
us	kākou, kāua

V

valley	awāwa
valuable	waiwai
various	likeʻole
victory, victorious	lanakila
visit	kipa

W

wait	kali
waiter/waitress	kuene
wall	paia
war	kaua
wash	holoi
to watch	nānā
watch	uaki
water	wai
wave	nalu, ʻale
weak	nāwaliwali

weave	ulana
Wednesday	pō'akolu
whisper	hāwanawana
white	ke'oke'o
wilted	mae
wind, breeze	makani
wise, educated	na'auao
wise saying	'ōlelo no'eau
woman	wahine
write	kākau
wrong	hewa

Y

yard	pā hale
year	makahiki
yellow	melemele
you	'oe
young	'ōpiopio
your	kou/kāu